The SKiLL-ionaire
in Every
Child

Boosting Children's Socio-Emotional Skills Using the Latest in Brain Research

Marie-Nathalie Beaudoin, Ph.D.

Dear Lori,

Thanks for your interest
and support of this work!

Marie Nathalie Beaudoin

oct 2010

Library of Congress Cataloging-in-Publication Data

Beaudoin, Marie-Nathalie
The SKiLL-ionaire in every child: Boosting children's socio-emotional skills using the latest in brain research

Includes bibliographical references.

ISBN 978-1-60910-476-4
1. Social skills (Psychology) 2. Emotional skills (Psychology)
3. Education

Printed in the United States of America.

Goshawk Publications
San Francisco, CA

To the children everywhere,
may you all get the opportunity to discover your inner wealth.
To my precious children,
may you keep your thoughtful and sunny view of life.
To my husband,
may you continue to see possibilities in everyone and everything.

CONTENTS

Preface

The *Skill-ionaire in Every Child* arises out of my professional work as a therapist practicing from a narrative therapy approach. It generally follows the legacy of the innovative work of Michael White and David Epston, who developed a markedly opposite view of therapeutic conversations from the one used in mainstream therapies. Instead of dwelling on problems, these two exceptional therapists deeply believed in people's abilities, and sought to bring forth the skills and wisdom of all through respectful and collaborative conversations. Adopting this approach myself in the 1990s, as a therapist in private practice and supervisor of school counseling services, I began to see people young and old emerge from under the cover of their problems and blossom into their best and preferred ways of being.

Then I became a mother...

From birth to age 7, my son was a poor sleeper, always struggling with nightmares and a number of fears. He was terribly shy, unable to talk to people outside of our nuclear family. We could never have a babysitter, leave him at a friend's house or birthday party. Any attempt to leave him with anyone else would trigger a powerful reaction of terror. My son was overly anxious and afraid of people. He was also fearful of heights, and a picky eater.

My husband and I felt so discouraged. I had spent my working life helping so many children and their families move away from complex emotional problems, and I couldn't even help my very own beloved son.

I spent many nights on the internet searching, searching, searching for something...as in addition to his excessive anxiety, I had two additional, small clues: he occasionally complained of headaches, and he sometimes reported that "his bones hurt." Not very often, but it stuck in my mind. Doctors said these were growth pains and didn't take them seriously. Neurologists and their MRIs found nothing.

I reluctantly started looking at food issues, and to make a very long story short, discovered that my son has celiac disease[1]. He had been living with a heightened biological level of anxiety and a full time, low grade headache, without knowing this sensation was abnormal since it had always been there. He only complained when it was unbearable. To my disbelief, within three weeks of eliminating gluten, dairy, and soy from his diet, I had a new child!

He became full of energy and playful, started talking to our neighbors (they had never heard his voice), being interested in making friends, and sleeping through the night. I now had a child open to the world, at last, and able to interact socially.... This was a glorious moment!

As these exciting weeks went by, I quickly realized however that the disease had left him with limited socio-emotional skills and unprepared to handle the friendships he now longed for.

---

[1] For more information on celiac disease, see the National Foundation for Celiac Awareness website at www.celiaccentral.org

How quickly can you make up a seven-year gap in practicing socio-emotional skills?

I started more deliberately using the ideas from narrative therapy in my parenting. In my more intimate role as a mother, I wondered how I could use the same therapeutic conversations that had proven so successful in my practice. What should I do differently?

I began engaging him in conversations that helped him notice what worked for him and others, socially and emotionally, in a variety of situations. Week after week, without pressure and very casually, I invited him gently into thinking about some situations he handled well and progressively helped him blossom into a well-rounded kid.

Excited by the results, I organized these ideas into a conversational map and started sharing them with other parents, refining my conversations with their children and adolescents, and blending in some concepts from neuroscience, mindfulness, and interpersonal neurobiology. I found the young people I worked with to be so knowledgeable! No matter what problem led to their consultation with me--anger, bullying, conflicts, shyness, jealousy, eating issues, depression--these kids had so many skills in facing their own problems. They just hadn't noticed their skills and realized how they could use them to make their lives different; that's where they needed a little help.

I was then invited to do some work with classrooms and found the results to be impressive even with large groups. The concept of "Skill Boosting" progressively emerged, and my analysis of research data on actual improvement of problem-solving skills in schools demonstrated that the approach worked. The more we discussed the children's successes following the map shared in this book, the more they expanded their thinking, their confidence, and their abilities to solve increasingly complex conflicts. This classroom work is in the process of being written into another book specifically for educators.

I am delighted to offer you *The Skill-ionaire in Every Child*. May fascinating conversations help *you* discover the incredible wealth of knowledge and skills hidden in skill-ionaire children in your own life.

Making
Big Problems Small
And
Small *People* *Big*

Introduction

Rita, 14, had struggled with depressive feelings, eating issues, self-doubt, self-cutting and insecurity around her friends. On a Monday morning she walks into her middle school, excited to wear her brand new, bright pink shoes. When the first girlfriend she meets says, "Ouch, those are the ugliest shoes I've ever seen," Rita calmly replies, "Well, I'm the one wearing them, so don't worry about it," and walks away maintaining her calm, coolness, and love of her shoes. How did this teenager go from being painfully insecure to so self-confident? Rita has experienced the power of Skill-Boosting Conversations (SBC), conversations that have deliberately increased her social and emotional intelligence using the latest scientific findings on the brain.

The last decade has seen an explosion of research in three fields: neuroscience, mindfulness, and positive psychology (Hanson & Mendius, 2009). We now know twice as much about the brain as we did twenty years ago because of the advent of revolutionary technologies such as MRI and fMRI, which allow us to see what's happening in people's brains. Scientists have made groundbreaking discoveries regarding the brain's ability to rewire (neuroplasticity) by demonstrating that training people to be fully aware of the present moment (mindfulness) can significantly *change* physiological structures of the brain, particularly the hippocampus, amygdala, and frontal lobes. What this means is that we can, literally, *train our own and our children's brain to respond differently to life.* These discoveries have led to a fantastic amount of writing on the biological correlates of emotions, memory, self-reflection, attachment and social interactions which have been integrated in the remarkable new science of interpersonal neurobiology (Siegel, 1999). At the same time, inspired by prominent psychologists such as White (2007), De Shazer (2005) and Seligman (2002), the field of psychology has finally shifted its century-old fascination with problems to an exploration of health, optimism, competency, and well-being.

Professionals in different fields have been grappling with the implications of these findings for parents, educators, and therapists. While some ideas have been put forth about how to enhance positive emotions, no one has yet proposed a conversational method applicable for parents, educators and counselors. *The Skill-ionaire in Every Child* offers a transformative conversational model I call "Skill-Boosting Conversations" (SBC), which draws directly on these exciting findings. The SBC approach was designed specifically to give parents, educators, and therapists new tools for fostering a deep and lasting optimism, reflection, self-worth, empathy, and compassion in young people's lives. Far more than a new gimmick, the SBC approach actually rewires the brain.

The SBC approach is unique in several key respects. Most current interventions, especially by parents and educators, involve a top-down process: adults teach young people what they should do. However this top-down approach has shown itself to be fraught with many problems, including the child's difficulty remembering what to do at critical times; its over-generalized, one-size-fits-all approach; and the fact that kids often find it just plain boring. SBC does exactly the opposite: it builds on a child's own successes, which are thoroughly and collaboratively examined with the adult; it is tailored to each child's unique life experience; and it keeps the child interested by deliberately focusing on what has worked successfully for the child thus far, as opposed to dwelling on problems. This powerful combination allows for the most complex level of neural encoding (or rewiring into the brain's circuitry) known to be possible.

Young people make decisions and deal with social or emotional dilemmas all the time. Ironically, perhaps, the more successful their responses, the more invisible these are to observers, who are more likely to notice problems or behavioral issues. Often without being aware of it, young people regularly generate incredibly clever ideas during the process of responding to tricky situations, whether they resolve the problem entirely, partially, or not at all. The SBC method focuses on these child-generated strategies by: 1. extracting the ingredients of successfully solved problems; 2. bringing young people's awareness to the existence of their strategies; 3. building on the implications of their successes, and 4. integrating the newly noticed skills into a sense of "skill-ionaire" identity, i.e. a sense of having a wealth of skills.

The Skill-ionaire in Every Child brings to light the natural genius of young people at coping and thriving through adversities and gives adults tools for strengthening these natural talents, whether their kids are struggling with anger, conflict, insecurities, fears, anxiety, trauma, social problems, body image or peer pressure. With its clear and practical approach, and its roots deep in the neuroscience of happiness, it offers the possibility of helping our kids move forward through life with confidence, competence, and compassion.

This book is written for adults wishing to make a difference in children's and adolescents' lives. It is my hope that parents, educators, and therapists will all find something that will be useful in their relationship with a young person.

For parents: SBC offer tools for consciously fostering children's self-confidence and self-competence. It allows them to ever so gently maximize the blooming of their child's potential while respecting their developmental readiness. Even three and four-year-olds can develop some competency in dealing with nightmares or avoiding tricky moments of sibling rivalry. Recent advances in neuroscience and interpersonal neurobiology have demonstrated that the small child's brain waits for experiences to determine how neural connections will be made. Parents who engage in brief SBC with their young children provide them with positive experiences of themselves as capable and therefore establish a stronger foundation for self-worth.

SBC provide parents of elementary-age children with a powerful method of supporting the fireworks of their emerging abilities on many levels: emotional, physical, social, and intellectual. The brains of elementary school-age children are bustling with activity. They are rapidly increasing their capacity for information-processing while also developing multiple forms of memory. Around the age of eight or nine, children also experience a striking growth of language, associative thinking, reasoning and inference of causes and effects.

Since cognitive stimulation makes a critical difference in brain development, parents who can help their children organize their thoughts and notice how they best control their impulses are laying helpful neural foundations for life.

Parents of adolescents will find that SBC enable their teenagers to be articulate and confident about the kind of people they prefer to be and much better able to deal with peer pressure, bullying, and the common social dramas of their group. Teens raised with SBC will more readily think about consequences before they act, exercise better judgment about their safety, and use their newly developed abstract thinking and deductive skills in proactive ways.

Teenagers who have been consciously and consistently encouraged to a keen awareness of their skills are also less vulnerable to the mood swings, episodes of self-doubt, high-risk behaviors, and eating issues that plague so many.

Finally SBC provide parents of teenagers a style of talking that encourages the sharing of personal information and creates a general home environment of trust and collaboration. This may sound too good to be true, given our predominant cultural assumption that rebellion and acting out are part of the teenage experience. Prepare to be surprised!

In sum, SBC allow parents to foster their children's mental development and experience rich, satisfying, and deeply intimate conversations with them.

For teachers: Teachers, principals, and educators, who have to cover a vast curriculum with a large group of youth while nurturing and helping each individual reach his/her potential, can easily become discouraged when relational or behavioral problems develop in their classrooms. Instead of trying to help teachers reduce problems, which can lead to further frustration, *The Skill-ionaire in Every Child* encourages the development of anti-problem skills. A teenager is far less likely to develop a bullying habit, for example, if the skills of empathy and compassion have been ingrained.

One of the advantages of the SBC approach is that it can be used with *all* students to foster sustained growth, whatever their developmental stage. For example, SBC can be used effectively in a classroom where a few students are starting to be disliked by their peers and maybe even falling into disrespectful behaviors. The SBC approach will make visible those times when these very students, as well as their classmates, refrain from mistreating others. Using real successes, each person can be invited into articulating all the reasons why they don't want to be hurtful, how they resist the temptation, what they tell themselves to contain their frustration and what they like about the outcome of their choice.

Such conversations can have many powerful effects. They make visible good intentions and efforts, which lead to an enhanced group appreciation; they actively expose all students to a number of youth-generated anger management ideas; they get students to know each other more intimately; and they provide the teacher an opportunity to model valuable, caring conversational skills.

For helping professionals: This book offers a conversational method to helping professionals, from counselors who meet regularly with young people, to tutors who may have just one meaningful conversation with a child. The beauty of SBC is that at times one conversation alone can leave behind glittering sparkles of competency in a young person's life. Experienced on a regular basis SBC have cumulative effects on the young person's sense of self-worth and confidence in many areas of life.

Counselors new to the field will appreciate having such an effective and respectful method that often produces meaningful changes. Experienced counselors will value the new skilled-based conversational possibilities presented by the book.

In sum, parents, teachers and helping professionals interested in supporting kids develop confidence, competence, and compassion can enrich children's lives through Skill-Boosting Conversations (SBC). Discovering *The Skill-ionaire in Every child* is life-transforming!

Book Overview
The book is divided into eight chapters. Chapter 1 invites readers to imagine how they would respond to the unexpected events in the lives of three different young people. Readers' typical responses are examined in terms of their intentions (usually well-meaning) and actual effects (often inadvertently negative). Some of the latest neuroscience findings on optimal learning context are then explained with their implications for alternative responses to problem situations. The concept of Skill-Boosting Conversations (SBC) is also introduced, with plenty of examples of real-life dialogues.

In chapter 2, I review the positive repercussions of SBC on four aspects of young people's development and relationships: 1. experience of conversations about a particular event (emotions and brain research involved, who's in the position of knowing, etc.); 2. sense of self (self-worth, self-confidence, logical thinking, responsibility and response-ability); 3. attitude towards others (empathy, awareness of others' intentions and goals, awareness of context, helpfulness); and 4. relationships with adults (power, intimacy, appreciation, and trust).

In chapter 3, six different types of responses to problems are presented. I explain how to extract the thinking strategies involved in the three problems that were successfully solved and look at the partially helpful ideas generated in the three unsolved problem scenarios. Different methods to engage in SBC for each of these situations are provided with examples and lively transcripts of conversations.

Chapter 4 discusses the existence of unnoticed treasures. Successes occur all the time, but it is simply impossible for any observer to see all of another person's successes, youth or adult, because we do not see the thinking inside their brain and do not oversee all of their activities. Getting young people to identify and share successes, especially those successes that occurred in our absence, can be very fruitful and exciting for parents, educators, and therapists. It is like searching a starry sky for a special galaxy or digging the earth for a precious treasure. You know there's probably something there, but the trick is to find it. Discovering unnoticed successes can be particularly difficult because they are encoded with a neutral or slightly positive emotion, which makes them less discernable.

Discovering these treasures requires artful questioning because young people forget and sometimes do not recognize a success as a success. Information gleaned from neuroscience and studies of memory are particularly useful for helping us extract forgotten or unnoticed successes. In this chapter, I point to some of the most useful data and current brain research on reactivating experiences that are embedded in neutral emotions. Examples of different conversations adults have had with children are used to illustrate the process. The chapter ends with an organized map to guide readers' explorations of successes.

In chapter 5, each small detail of information about an event is discussed as being like a building block, like an "experiential lego". You can leave experiential blocks scattered on the floor of the mind, use them to build a cage by focusing on the problematic aspects of the event, or use them to progressively build a museum of valuable treasures. In this chapter, readers are offered concrete practices that allow them to use "experiential legos" to enhance young people's emotional and social intelligence.

While emotional intelligence is enriched when young people are invited to notice that they are capable of solving problems, social intelligence requires consideration of a more complex set of factors. The particular factors examined in the SBC of this chapter are: initial thinking, the dual consideration of self and others, and the resulting implications. The metaphor of an airplane flying *over* a conflict rather than plunging into it is used to illustrate these concepts. The goal is to associate a detailed awareness of the helpful thoughts and actions with an awareness of the multiple positive ramifications. This chapter is especially full of information on how to facilitate these conversations respectfully and what to avoid. The entertaining story of a very athletic teenager being required to attend a lengthy poetry reading with his mother and sister provides an example of the conversational process extracting the social and emotional skills used. Once identified, these skills become more meaningful and usable for this young man.

Chapter 6 is the living heart of the book. It describes how to move a young person from having a collection of various skills to becoming a calm, confident, optimistic, and compassionate person. These characteristics are developed by the repetitive focus on particular aspects of successful problem solving.

Specifically, young people progressively become trained to: 1. be aware of and detached from their own thinking (*meta-awareness*); and 2. develop a broader perspective of themselves, the situation, and other people (*"invisibles"*).

Young people are trained to develop meta-awareness by becoming increasingly aware of the complex and contradictory thoughts that cross their minds in difficult situations. While discussing successes, they are encouraged to recognize how experience is usually multifaceted and to name the different parts of themselves. These parts often end up being discussed metaphorically as parts of their brain, for example the part of your brain that helps you stay patient while another part may be getting annoyed.

As the awareness of their thought process increases, so does their sense of agency and the recognition that they have choices when faced with a tricky situation. If a young person becomes aware of a preference for calm, for example, she will discover that she can search for her "calm part" when responding to events. In other words, the awareness allows her to activate her own brain's firing for calm.

Readers are then introduced to the idea of "invisibles", those important contextual factors that influence people's behaviors, often without their notice. Someone's "invisibles" may include being hungry, having had a bad day, being worried about a karate test, being sick, having forgotten their lunch, etc... They include all the personal experiences that may inadvertently render a person more impatient or more prone to being unpleasant. Recognizing the presence of "invisibles" increases young people's ability to experience empathy and compassion.

For example, it is difficult to get upset at a peer's impatience when you know his beloved dog passed away yesterday.

The process of acknowledging "invisibles" is powerful because there are always more solutions to problems in a big picture understanding than in the narrow view of an event. The process of acknowledging "invisibles" is also powerful because it reduces the roller coaster of emotions and allows for a compassionate understanding of the needs of oneself and others. When young people see more of the problem in the context, they see more of the peer in the person.

Contrary to popular beliefs, even young children can benefit from this method. In spite of their self-centeredness and developing brains, they can be empowered to develop meta-awareness and to consider invisibles. What makes this possible is the fact that these conversations "bathe" the child in successes and positive emotions. Children eventually become who they practice to be, and the SBC method creates opportunities for reviewing and practicing their very best and skilled ways of being.

In chapter 7, I review the scientific benefits of helping the young people in our lives to become competent, self-confident, calm, optimistic, and compassionate. This includes a number of health benefits, experience of happiness, academic performance, multiple relationships, and others. Young people who develop these ways of being also display some abilities typically learned in mindfulness trainings. All young people can feel like skill-ionaires when regularly invited into an awareness of their own social and emotional intelligence.

Chapter 8 discusses the use of SBC when young people are struggling with a socio-emotional problem. Special considerations must be taken into account before engaging in SBC. Additional ways of engaging in helpful conversations are discussed and illustrated with a number of examples.

Finally the book concludes with a review of the SBC method and the end of Rita's story.

CHAPTER 1

Three Basic Beliefs about Skills

Late afternoon, nine-year-old Mike and his friend were playing by the river while their parents set up the campsite. After a few moments the parents realized that the boys were gone! Apparently they had decided to go either up or downstream without asking or informing anyone. Their parents felt this was unsafe and were upset by their lack of consideration. After an hour and a half of worry, the boys returned, unaware of the distress they had caused.

In a 3rd grade class, students were supposed to write a comment on each other's planet project poster board. Sam refused to write any comment on the board of his well-known class enemy.

Shelly, 14, ran away for three days, the longest she'd ever done this. Everyone was worried about her safety and where she could possibly be. When she finally came back, everybody was very angry. Her parents took many privileges away and the school decided this was the last straw. She wouldn't be allowed to walk at graduation.

How would you respond to these situations?

Adults' intentions

Immediately after hearing each of these true stories, most adults have some ideas about what they would like to say to the youth involved. It is assumed that if a young person engages in what is perceived as a problem-behavior, then he or she probably needs to *learn* something. Adults--whether parents, educators, or counselors--further assume that it is our job to teach the young person to think or behave differently than she or he does. We want to do our job, as responsible adults, of "coaching," "raising," "educating," "protecting," or "fostering the growth" of those under our care.

In fact, the more we care, the more we want young people to learn to think and act differently in the face of problems, and the more we are compelled to make visible why the behavior was objectionable and what should have been done differently. While counselors may attempt to accomplish this goal by discussing the problem in depth, parents and educators tend to give some kind of consequence, such as the removal of a privilege, hoping that a little suffering will enhance learning.

Regardless of our varied roles, the ultimate goal behind most adults' responses is to teach young people to:
- **think** about the implications of their choice next time
- **grow** by examining their mistakes
- **develop skills** to make better choices.

Adults' effects
In many of these problem situations, adults' typical questions, talks, or consequences do not have the intended effects. Counselors' talking and asking questions about a problem may create a context where the young person shuts down, answers with a lot of "I don't know," or becomes defensive. Parents' and educators' consequence giving may lead to a build-up of resentment. Consequences that make sense to

the young person and are given only occasionally, without damaging the adult-youth relationship, can be effective in fostering learning sometimes. Research shows, however, that consequences and punishments, especially the big ones, most often lead to resentment, hatred and a perception that adults are mean (Kohn, 1999).

During timeouts, young people aren't in their rooms thinking about what they could have done better. They are usually brooding resentment and anger.

In effect, our attempts to correct the problem can end up tripling it instead: first came the objectionable behavior, second the anger or defensiveness, and third a damaged relationship.

Advances in neuroscience also clearly demonstrate that the higher cortical functions required for complex learning shut down when an individual is experiencing defensiveness, fear or anger (Siegel, 1999; Bluestein, 2008). This means that we fail over and over again at associating a problem behavior with reflection, understanding, and more appropriate responses. The young person's memory does not associate the behavior with the lesson. Such a deduction would involve the logic-oriented frontal cortex. Instead the more primitive limbic system is engaged and the *adult* becomes labeled as a cause of emotional discomfort.

Is there a more brain-compatible way of accomplishing the intended effect of cultivating socio-emotional skills?

Advances in neuroscience have demonstrated consistently (Damasio, 1994; LeDoux, 1996; Sousa, 2001) that the optimal learning environment is one where three experiences occur simultaneously:

1. a positive emotion
2. exposure to personally relevant information
3. interest, excitement, or curiosity

In other words, the brain encodes its most complex and lasting knowledge when people experience a pleasant feeling coupled with a discussion of something that is both meaningful and gratifying. This is well described by Daniel Siegel (2009, p.16):

"The experiences we provide as teachers--or as parents or therapists--focus students' (children's or patients') attention, activate their brain, and create the possibility of harnessing neural plasticity in those specific areas. Coupled with emotional engagement, a sense of novelty and optimal attentional arousal, teaching with reflection can utilize these prime conditions for building new connections in the brain."

Is it possible to help young people think better and talk about their mistakes in a way that would elicit such excitement, meaning, and interest? Is it possible to have a conversation about problems where the young person would not become defensive or shut down but rather engaged and interested in what adults have to say? Is it possible to have conversations in which young people are encouraged to cultivate social and emotional skills that they would then be comfortable and confident using when faced with problems again?

YES!!!

Skill Boosting Conversations (SBC) offer a method of investigating situations that elicit all three of the brain's optimal learning components. The very process of SBC reactivates neural connections of the areas associated with successful problem solving in a way that can transform a possibly random and temporary state into a long-term trait of the young person. Uncovering young people's very own productive thinking automatically provides them with experiences of competency, excitement, and interest.

Allow me to illustrate this process with the stories introduced above. While all of the problems described were of concern to caring adults, they were all, ironically, incredible stories of successes at thinking and problem solving. This thinking and solving occurred in a blurry, improvised way that was not fully articulated by the young people involved. The thinking was very brittle and was likely to be buried and forgotten under the weight of any anger or resentment generated by interactions with adults. Yet this reasoning was a treasure worth digging for, in the name of cultivating thinking skills. Let's look at how we might use Skill Boosting Conversations (SBC) in these situations and then discuss the three principles guiding the process.

1. A problem doesn't mean a lack of skills

Adults often think that, if a child makes a mistake, or has a problem, it implies a deficit in their thinking or their skills. Is that really true? When you find yourself yelling at someone, is it because you do not know how to be calm?

Problems with young people do not necessarily mean that they are lacking a skill or need our teaching. As the mother of Mike in story #1, I was tempted to lecture the boys about all the possible dangers of drowning in the deeper parts of the river, getting lost, the late time of the day, and not warning any adult of their departure. Instead I took a deep breath and engaged in the following conversation with my son:

MN: Mike, what do you think about you two going away like that?

Mike: It wasn't a good idea...

MN: What makes you think it wasn't a good idea?

Mike: Well, we hadn't told anyone where we were, and we hadn't really planned to go that far, but we really went too far. We were just looking for crawdads. We first went downriver and since it was really deep we decided it would be safer to turn around and go the other way where the water was only knee deep. So we came back and then went the other way a little. But then we tried catching some fish that were swimming away and that took us further.

MN: How did you decide to come back in the end?

Mike: Well, I could tell the light in the sky was changing and my feet were cold and it had been a long time since we were gone. I really wanted to turn around.

MN: Did Lance understand that?

Mike: Yes, but he wanted to come back by a trail in the forest. We had a discussion. I was afraid we would get lost. I, for sure, was coming back the way we came because I knew for sure it would take us to the campsite.

MN: So you thought that you could have gotten lost coming back a different way? What did you think about specifically?

Mike (thinking): Well, it was late...we really didn't have much time to try different ways, and if we had gotten lost in

*the forest we had no water, no food, there were coyotes ...
and bears ...and ... mountain lions maybe...and you
wouldn't know where to look for us! It would have been
really scary. Wow, I'm so glad I insisted on coming back the
river way.*

*MN: Getting lost would have been scary! So you were able
to think about the time of day, the dangers with wild animals,
the lack of supplies, and the fact we wouldn't be able to find
you?*

*Mike: Yeah! I also thought it would be safer for us to stay
together so I convinced him to come my way.*

*MN: So you also thought of the importance of staying
together?*

*Mike: Yeah...then we can help each other out if something
happens.*

*MN: You thought of a lot of things! But you know we were
also worried...Might you want to explore the river differently
next time?*

*Mike: Oh yeah! ... I'd really prefer if a grown-up came with
us. I was nervous. I don't want to do that again.*

After this conversation, Mike most likely did a bit more
thinking on his own. If instead I had peppered him with
questions about the multiple facets of the problem, or delivered
a lecture or punishment, that would likely have hijacked his
attention towards either the consequence itself or the anger he
would have experienced. The problem solving, which he
actually did engage in, would have been stampeded not
strengthened.

By the time the conversation was completed, Mike had
thought about all the items of concern to adults and much more!
I was left impressed and appreciative of his thinking. He was

left feeling more determined not to do this again, proud of his problem-solving abilities, and most importantly, on the same team with his parents about his safety.

2. Important efforts and skills are often hidden: Examine the problem-solving process not just the outcome

There is so much we don't know about what happens in a young person's mind. Most of the time parents, counselors, and educators' inferences about children's thinking are biased by our own view of the world as adults and consequently our solutions to problems do not even fit the intricacies of the young person's life. Asking gentle questions from a place of kind curiosity and interest will reveal fascinating information and complex thinking that is completely unpredictable (White, 2007). Respectful questions may even reveal that what looked like a problem to the observing adult was actually a successful attempt at avoiding a bigger issue.

In story #2, the third-grade student had been participating in a SBC classroom project and had gained some experience in noticing and articulating his successes.

Sam (coming to me): MN, I think I maybe had a success today but I'm not sure.
MN (interested): Really, tell me about it.
Sam: I'm so angry Eva wrote a mean comment about my planet project.
MN: What did she write?
Sam (resentful): She wrote "Whaaaat??" like she thought it was a crappy project.
MN: So you took that as a criticism?

Sam: Yeah, she hates me, everyone knows we're enemies.
MN: So what did you do?
Sam: I asked her why she wrote that but she just shrugged and walked away.
MN: She shrugged and walked away? Was that upsetting?
Sam: Yeah, I thought of saying something mean but I didn't.
MN (curious): You didn't say anything mean?
Sam: No, and then I thought of writing something really, really mean on her project...but I didn't want to do that...
MN: You didn't want to do that? What kept you from doing that?
Sam (thinking): I don't know....Euh...I guess I didn't want to do that, because then I'd be just like her. I thought it would be more mature to not do that.
MN: So you thought it would be more mature. What did you do to avoid writing a mean comment?
Sam: I tried to stay away from her project and do all the other ones, slowly, hoping I would not have time to comment on hers. And it worked, I didn't have time for hers'!
MN: You stayed away and it worked! Was that hard to stay away from her project?
Sam: Oh yeah...
MN: Was there anything that you were thinking that helped you stay away from her project?
Sam: I'm not sure...
MN: What may have been going around in your mind while you stayed away from her project?
Sam (thinking): I thought everyone would think that I'm the one who's mean and then I might get in trouble. I didn't want that.
MN: You thought of what would happen after, like the consequences sort of?

Sam (slowly): Yeah, I thought I would be the strongest if I didn't write anything mean and not writing at all seemed like the lowest mean I could do.

MN: So if you actually had to write something it would have been hard to resist the temptation to write a mean comment while not writing at all was the safest way to stay at the lowest mean possible?

Sam (smiling): Yeah!

MN: Wow, how do you call that part of you that helped you think of the lowest mean strategy and the consequences?

Sam (proud): The mature part of me! I think I like to be mature!

No observing adult could have guessed this behavior represented a success rather than a problem! Sadly, in many schools, a refusal like Sam's would have lead to conflicts with the teacher. Fortunately for this student, the teacher was flexible, which made it safe for him to experiment with creative problem solving. Under the appearance of a problem, Sam's refusal to evaluate his peer was in reality an extraordinary success. Only gentle questions and an openness to hearing young people's experiences could make that visible and a trampoline for growth such as acknowledging that one can be, and likes to be, mature.

3. Broadening our scope from a problem to a skill focus: Meaningful learning can occur in the absence of problem talk

Problem behaviors can be so big and serious that they often blind adults to everything else. This was the case with Shelly's situation. Certainly the habit of running away when there was a conflict at home was serious and needed to be addressed.

Addressing it head on however was not a wise idea. It is often preferable to start with a skill boosting conversation and then later, if needed, gently attempt to make strides about the problem. In this story, as in many others, the visible behavior is only the tip of the iceberg. The most important part of the solution is hidden and can only be revealed through respectful conversation.

Shelly: Everyone is so mean, I shouldn't have come back.
MN: What made you decide to come back?
Shelly: I didn't want to live like a runaway anymore.
MN: You didn't want to live like that anymore? How would you like to live?
Shelly: I'd like to have a real job, make money and have more freedom… not just run all the time.
MN: So you'd like to have a job, make money and have freedom. Do you have a specific dream?
Shelly: Yeah…I'd like to be a cook.
MN: To be a cook?
Shelly: Yeah, I've always liked to cook and I'm good at it too!
MN: Where did you learn to cook?
Shelly: My grandma used to cook with me before she died.
MN: What would your grandma say, if she could, about your dream of being a cook?
Shelly (smiling): She'd be real' pleased!
MN: Would she be pleased if you stopped running away too?
Shelly: Yeah, she'd want me to get my act together.
MN: Did thinking of your grandma also help you come back?
Shelly: Not really but now I think it would.
MN: What difference would it make?
Shelly: It would help me hang in there through the tough times 'cause she was tough.

MN: So your grandma was tough. Did you have to be tough too to come back?
Shelly: Yeah, I knew everyone would be mad and I really hesitated. I could have gone somewhere really cool with some friends but in the end I decided not to…
MN: Was there anything other than your dream of being a cook and having a real job and freedom that helped you come back?
Shelly: Yeah, I thought of my little brother and how hard it would be on him if I didn't come back for good.
MN: So thinking of your little brother…do you care about him?
Shelly: Yeah…I do…and things are pretty hard for him too…
MN: Are there things you can teach him about being tough, having dreams and making life better for himself? (nods) How does one go about being tough?

The conversation goes on about her little brother, grandma, parents, her dream for herself and the other reasons she came back[2]. The point of this example however is that the reasons she returned were much more important to emphasize than giving her consequences even though the problem was serious. While the adults involved were well intended, wanted her to learn and never run away anymore, their actions had just the opposite effect of making her doubt the decision of coming back. Our SBC strengthened and further enriched her desire to stop running away, left her with a positive feeling of competency, connection to her family and a sense that …coming back was not such a bad decision after all!

---

[2] Being a clinical psychologist, I also have the responsibility of inquiring about the safety of my clients. This was done in this situation and the family was invited for family therapy sessions. Those aspects of the work however are not relevant to this particular book.

Questions and answers

Question: Isn't focusing on successes and being appreciative of children's efforts, similar to praise and reinforcement?

Answer. I can see how they might seem similar, but there are major differences that will become more and more apparent as you read the book. In a nutshell, when you're praising:

- The adult takes most of the airtime emotionally and verbally
- The child is listening passively
- The content of the conversation is something that pleases the adult.

In SBC, it is exactly the opposite:

- The adult refrains from being overly expressive and only asks gentle questions
- The young person is active: the brain is much more involved when one is thinking and answering questions
- The content of the conversation is something the youth is pleased with and interested in sharing.

Question. Do Skill Boosting Conversations really make a significant difference?

Answer. Yes! SBC have many desirable effects, which we will begin to examine in the next chapter. A variety of SBC are also possible depending on the goal. It can take some time to figure out what questions to ask, and as you probably noticed in the above dialogues, I chose questions that were particularly relevant to their stories. In story number one, I extracted the child's ability to think of risks and solve problems. In story number two, I emphasized the child's success at thinking about consequences and the kind of person he wanted to be; and in story number three, I reconnected the teenager to a preferred identity which included her future dreams for herself and a sense of connection to family members.

The variety of possible SBC will be explained in more depth in chapters 3 and 4. For now, the complex ramifications of SBC will be discussed so that you can become fully informed of what you are getting into.

CHAPTER 2

Do Skill Boosting Conversations Really Make a Difference?

Skill Boosting Conversations (SBC) make significant differences on many levels. Those effects can be more easily understood by comparing this type of conversation to the more traditional skill teaching process. By skill teaching, I mean the common way in which well-intentioned adults ask questions about "problems" or conflicts, tell young people what they should have done, why they shouldn't have done what they did, or discuss all the consequences that follow from their questionable choice. Once again I would like to underscore that this teaching is usually done from a place of caring about the young person and wanting to do our job as adults to "educate," "counsel," or "help" those under our care. SBC offer another way of fostering growth that can often better accomplish our goal. In the sections that follow, I will contrast skill teaching to skill boosting on the:

1. Conversational process (who's describing what happened, whose knowledge is given higher value, which emotions are involved, recent brain research)
2. Implications for young people's sense of self (self-worth, self-confidence, logical thinking, responsibility, and response-ability)
3. Effects on young people's attitude towards others (empathy, awareness of others' intention and goals, awareness of context, helpfulness)

4. Effects on the adult-youth relationship (power, intimacy, appreciation, and trust)

Conversational process

The act of putting words to experiences

Putting words to experiences and speaking them articulates thoughts that would otherwise remain blurry. There is even evidence from neuroscience that this process of labeling experiences balances the activity of the left and right hemispheres in a way that allows for a better integration of the experience (Siegel, 2007).

In skill teaching conversations, young people often find themselves defending what they did, i.e. the problem behavior. In our chapter 1 stories, for example, if questioned, lectured or punished, the river-exploring boys would likely have defended themselves by explaining how they weren't paying attention and just went from one part of the river to another without realizing what they were doing. Their carelessness and inattentiveness would have been the focus of attention, leaving them feeling rather foolish. In our second story, if Sam had been confronted by a teacher, parent or counselor, he would have been forced to justify how mean Eva had been and how upset he was, which may simply have heightened the anger and the animosity between the two students. In story number 3, had she been challenged by adults, Shelly would have justified why she ran away, become increasingly clear about and committed to her reasons, and further connect to the unhappiness of her situation. This would leave her more than ever tempted to run away again.

In many situations (not all obviously), a teaching attitude inadvertently worsens the actual problem and leaves young people less able to make better choices in the future.

In SBC, as was illustrated in the earlier transcripts, young people articulate the useful thoughts that simmered in their minds. In this process they revisit the event and automatically reconsolidate its memory, enriching it with problem-solving strategies and increased positive emotions. A memory is simply a group of neurons firing together. When we activate this network of firing neurons (the memory of a successful event) and talk about it in a skill boosting way, new neurons are co-activated and automatically associated with the original memory (Fields, 2005). As a result, when it goes back into storage in the brain, the original memory becomes infused with an experience of agency and positive emotions. Progressively, with repetitive SBC, young people are changing the scenery of their brains where problematic situations may yet maintain some of their unpleasant charge, but they are mediated by an experience of skills and competency.

Knowledge

In traditional skill teaching conversations, adults often do a lot of the talking and young people are expected more or less to listen. Adults generate questions, ideas, solutions, teach a skill and explain what is problematic in what they see. They base the conversation on what they saw or what other observers told them. Usually adults will try to influence the young person not to do this again or to choose a different behavior…The young person becomes a passive recipient of the adult's thoughts about the event.

Inadvertently, these talks can also become fundamentally intellectual and disconnected from what it's really like to walk in the young person's shoes. Many young people will report, for example, that they got in trouble because they were not "respectful." When asked what being "respectful" means, they often don't really know, even if the adult explained the issue over and over again! There's a mismatch in language and thinking process that is difficult to bridge partly because the brains of adults and youth are fairly different and don't process information in the same way (Bjork & al, 2004), and partly because there is a lot that we adults don't see.

In SBC the starting point is the young people's own experience of events. They are the only ones who really know what happened and what shaped their responses. They certainly are the only ones who have access to what happened in their minds and hearts, what they were thinking and feeling, and what they were paying attention to. Very often they are the ones to know about the details of the history between themselves and the person with whom they had conflict, as in the story of Sam and his "well-known enemy".

Conversational possibilities are much broader as young people actively reveal information that could never have been guessed by adults. This occurred for example in the story of Mike, regarding his friend's idea of coming back a different way. Young people are the bearers of knowledge about their own experience. Adults only facilitate an exploration of what took place and uncover ideas or thoughts that contributed to the successful unfolding of the solution.

Most young people, and frankly many adults, will experience a complex jumble of thoughts and feelings, and respond with little awareness of what exactly transpired so successfully. In fact, research has shown that a person can speak at a rate of 160 words per minute while the brain is actually able to process about 800 words per minute (Joesting & al., 1996). A lot of important invisible activity is happening in the brain that is unseen to observers and not necessarily even known to the brain's owner! This is where adults can be most helpful: in unraveling piece by piece the components of the successful problem-solving *experience*. In that sense, the starting point of the learning process is experiential in nature.

Brain relevance

In skill teaching conversations, adults attempt to "implant" new behaviors and thoughts into young people's brain. While this form of teaching may, at times, be unavoidable and even necessary, its success is necessarily limited because it doesn't give us the same level of access to the brain's natural learning powers. Studies show that after three days young people retain only an average of 10% of what was taught in a lecture style (Moore, 2005). As we discussed earlier, skill teaching is limited in scope by virtue of the intellectual nature of the material, the neutral or uncomfortable emotions triggered and the limited interest of the young person.

The brain is fundamentally an experience-encoding device (Siegel, 1999). It is designed to sort, understand, memorize, and learn from *what we live,* and this is particularly true for young people, for whom the frontal cortex is not fully developed. In general, the brain encodes a lot more than we are aware of. You can be in a restaurant, for example, and not pay attention to the fact that the person at the next table is reading a book. Yet prompted skillfully about it at a later time, you would be able to remember that detail.

A classic study conducted by National Training Laboratories found that we remember 10-20% of what we hear, 30% of what we see demonstrated, 50% of what we discuss and 75% of what we experience, practice, or teach (National Training Laboratories of Bethel, 1960). Imagine the incredible amount of details the brain encodes with each second of lived experience! A very complex and rich web of electrical firing retrieves past memories, creates new ones, links emotions and thoughts, analyzes sensory inputs and outputs, makes assumptions, and creates responses. Why cultivate skills with any other material than what's already richly encoded *in* the brain?

In Mike's story again, the discussion involving his own lived experience of concern regarding the possibility of being lost will be encoded in his memory and remembered much more fully than any lecture on safety a parent could have given upon his return. The best possible conversational material is right there in the very thinking of the young person's brain. Mike made some valuable decisions and was at least partially successful at solving his problem, leaving a canvas of experience in the form of a neural pathway. The next step is to connect and enrich this existing neural pathway with higher cortical functions such as meta-thinking (thinking about your thinking), awareness of self, others, context, and to make meaning of what happened in a future, usable way.

In sum, as indicated in the table below, SBC is associated with a much greater learning potential.

Table 2.1: Summary of the conversational process

	Skill Boosting Conversations focus on success	**Skill Teaching Conversations** focus on problem
What is articulated	The helpful skills	The problem
Who's knowledgeable	The young person	The adult
Type of knowledge	Experiential	Intellectual
Participation level in the conversation	Young person is generally actively contributing	Young person is more or less passive or defensive
Focus	Assets	Deficits
Content	The invisible thought process (cannot be seen)	The visible behavior or action (what was seen)
Interest in conversation	Moderate to High	Minimal to Moderate
Conversation possibilities	Rich with unexpected details being added	Thin or limited in scope by the focus of the adult
Brain relevance	Existing neural pattern reinforced in powerful ways	Requires working to create a new neural network
Connection to life experience	Maximized as the incident is relevant to personal life	Minimal to moderate as the discussion may feel irrelevant
Emotion	Positive	Negative or neutral

2. Effects on the young person's sense of self

Effects on self-worth

In traditional skill teaching conversations, young people are far more vulnerable to feeling uncomfortable or incompetent. In the name of learning, they are forced to put their nose in the worst aspects of their actions. Because the adults do not notice their efforts and successes, these young people can end up attributing their problems to internal deficiencies and seeing their successes as being the results of luck (Dweck, 2005). Such explanatory style has been associated with a tendency toward depression and helplessness later in life (Seligman, 2002).

By giving attention to these skills, by noticing them and valuing them, SBC help children and adolescents attribute their successes to their abilities. Since young people see themselves through others' eyes (White & Epston, 1990), being appreciated by an adult for their clever thinking invariably gives them a profound sense of self-worth. This was the case, for example, in Sam's story, where he ended up determining that he had been "mature" and "liked it." The adult's simple act of acknowledging, validating and helping him recognize this preferred way of being had a big impact.

In some of these conversations, young people are also placed in the position of actually sharing these skills with those who are interested or who can benefit from them. This was the case for Shelly when she was invited to share some of her helpful ideas with her little brother. As discussed earlier, explaining one's skills to another can be a powerful experience for young people and is another proof that their ideas are worthy.

Effects on self-confidence

By contrast, skill teaching conversations can leave young people feeling embarrassed and incompetent. These uncomfortable states make it more difficult to take the risk of trying out the new behaviors suggested by adults. This would be particularly true in situations of conflict where young people's brain are infused with intense emotions such as anger or hurt which automatically reduces their frontal lobe's ability to recall intellectual teachings. (Sousa, 2006).

One of the more striking outcomes of SBC is that young people become very articulate about the specific skills that serve them best. They are able to name them, know first-hand how they personally engage in them, have a deep understanding of why and how they work, and believe in their ability to be successful using these skills. Young people's deep awareness of having mastered these powerful skills, allows them to be more confident in tackling challenging situations. Their perception of their ability is heightened and they are more able to be calm when facing challenges. They become more response-able, that is, able to respond in a constructive manner (Covey, 2004). Sam, for example, now knows that he can be upset at his "class enemy" and still behave in the "mature" way he prefers.

Effects on self-reflection

Another characteristic of skill teaching conversations is that it does little to encourage self-reflection, and even when it does, it's usually confined in intellectually structured framework. For example, children can be taught to make "I statements" (instead of "you hurt me," they might be asked to say, "I was hurt when …"), which require them to rephrase what they said using language in which they take responsibility for their own feelings instead of blaming. While this may be useful to highlight a constructive phraseology, it usually has a limited impact on their ability to self-reflect and is unlikely to be remembered during a heated conflict. As mentioned earlier, when intense emotions are present, the significantly reduced activity of the frontal lobe inhibits the recall of intellectual lessons.

SBC's starting point is self-reflection. Young people are constantly invited to notice and examine the thinking involved in their successes. Since the process is rooted in positive emotions, young people appreciate the experience and eventually start engaging in self-reflection on their own. Being able to "see" what is arising in one's mind builds many of the same skills developed by mindfulness meditation practitioners, such as insight and awareness (Wallace, 2007). Such skills have been shown to enable the development of the middle prefrontal regions and insular cortex, promoting self-regulatory and executive functions of the brain (Lazar, et al., 2005). As well stated by Daniel Siegel (2007, p.266), "With reflection, students are offered a neural capacity to socially, emotionally, and academically approach life with resilience. What a gift for a healthy development".

Effects on ability to think of consequences

Adults tend to invite young people to think of the consequences of their behaviors only when they make mistakes. As discussed earlier, because of the way our brains are wired, such learning is often biologically hampered by the presence of uncomfortable emotions such as defensiveness, anger or fear of punishment (LeDoux, 1996).

In contrast, SBC, focusing as it does on helpful thinking or successful actions (as will be discussed in the next chapter), offer particularly fertile grounds for highlighting the rippling effects of one's choice. Young people may even rejoice in thinking about all of the positive effects that their choice had. In fact the more positive effects, the more excitement and pride at having accomplished *all* of that! In the meantime various categories of effects can be explored, such as effects on self, other people, relationship to other people, how they see you, the unfolding events of the day, the amount of fun, your access to privileges, etc.

Mike had just such an opportunity to consider consequences when he thought of the implications of getting lost in the forest. The conversation made visible the specific categories of consequences (effects on one's emotions, health, relationships, etc...) to make them more easily memorable. While many other categories of consequences could have been explored, it didn't seem necessary in that context.

With each conversation, various categories of consequences become more and more practiced and programmed in the brain. In fact, young people who have participated in SBC have been shown to develop an ability to think of consequences that goes beyond what is deemed possible by many neurologists and developmental psychologists.

Responsibility and response-ability

Responsibility is generally defined as the ability to think and act in a reliable and accountable way. Covey (2004) has expanded this general view to highlight that a truly responsible person is actually "response-able" meaning capable of making decisions informed by an awareness of self, others, and possibilities. As discussed earlier, in the traditional skill teaching conversations, young people often do not fully integrate the intellectual lessons adults are trying to teach them. They may feel inadequate, unskilled and one down in a hierarchical relationship with adults. If they make a mistake, it can be tempting to hide it, especially if they sense a potential consequence or anticipate an uncomfortable conversation. Instead of becoming more responsible, these children and adolescents will often end up worried about displeasing adults. The discomfort of both being instructed to do something one doesn't totally get and the sense of being inadequate reduces the likelihood of being aware of oneself, others, and creative possibilities. The brain becomes mostly preoccupied with shutting down uncomfortable feelings and protecting oneself (Damasio, 1994).

When young people are regularly engaged in the process of exploring their own successes, they tend to cultivate and expand a triple awareness of self, others, and possibilities. The satisfaction they gain by skillfully resolving problems further motivates them to continue acting in ways that lead to positive outcomes. In this process, young people become more and more committed to engaging with others in personally and socially appreciated ways. They become more responsible and response-able. At the same time, the adults in their lives, having witnessed and appreciated the thinking process of such young people, are more likely to consider them reliable and accountable. Again, because young people tend to see themselves through other people's eyes, experiencing the positive response from adults confirms their feeling of competency and abilities to be responsible.

In sum, SBC is associated with a more complex set of learning outcomes, as indicated in the table below.

Table 2.2: Summary of implications on experience of self

	Skill Boosting Conversations focus on success	**Skill Teaching Conversations** focus on problem
Effects on self-worth	Young people feel more capable and competent	Young people feel inadequate, unskilled, having to learn
Effects on self-confidence	Boosts it	Diminishes it
Effects on self-reflection	Enhanced and appreciated	Limited and structured
Improvement in problem solving skills	Young people are more articulate in strategies that are a good fit for them	Need to practice, may not succeed in applying an intellectual concept at a high emotional time
Commitment to using the strategy	Maximized, as young people know their strategies work, trust that they can do it and are more committed to it because it is their idea	Minimized, as young people may be unsure if it'll work and may not fully understand how to do it

(continued)	**Skill Boosting Conversations** focus on success	**Skill Teaching Conversations** focus on problem
Effects on ability to notice the consequences of choices	High	Low
Effects on responsibility	Able to think and act in a more reliable way	Young people may attempt to hide their mistakes
Effects on response-ability	Increased as young people notice over and over again their abilities and learn to trust themselves	Young people often do not feel better equipped to respond

3. Effects on the attitude toward others

Empathy and awareness of others' feelings

Many adults resent or become angry at young people's seeming inability to experience compassion for others' feelings, especially when a conflict occurs. Attempting to teach young people to understand and feel the suffering of another young person, especially during a conflict, is often quite a losing battle. Moreover, forcing young people to apologize against their will only feeds their resentment and sabotages the genuine regrets that may come later. In such situations, empathy for the other person is usually blocked by the young person's own negative experience. It should be said that in more neutral situations, young people who are developmentally ready can experience empathy, although it may be biased by some self-centeredness (Eisenberg & Morris, 2004).

In SBC, the adult invites the young person to examine what she spontaneously notices about others. This exploration will often extend into an increasingly complex observation of others' thoughts, feelings, and contexts. In other words, young people first discover their own awareness of others and then are progressively encouraged to pay attention to different aspects of others' experiences. Once again this strengthens the brain's neural pathway for empathy in a way that suits the person's unique developmental level.

Awareness of others' intentions and goals

Very often, when adults wish to discuss a conflict, the young people involved will typically claim that the other did it "on purpose" or because they're "mean!" It can be very difficult to convince them to consider any other hypothesis or to teach them to have a broader perspective. The anger and resentment they experienced is effectively blocking their neural capacity to "put themselves in the other person's shoes."

For this reason, it can be extremely valuable to use SBC to get young people to examine the more constructive hypotheses they generate about other people's intentions when they have successfully solved a social dilemma. We'll discuss using SBC about situations that are 100% successful in our next chapter. Those types of conversations are very useful to expand the young person's perspective on others' point of view and intentions. This process is facilitated by the positive feelings experienced and a greater openness to thinking about others, which provide the young person with a broader repertoire of possibilities for understanding human behavior.

Awareness of context

Skill teaching conversations tend to focus mainly on behaviors and ignore context. As we will see later in this book, an understanding of context is essential to solve problems, and foster compassion in many social interactions (Beaudoin & Taylor, 2009). It is quite simple to introduce considerations of context into SBC.

Helpfulness

Helpfulness and altruism are two virtues often emphasized, both in religious institutions and at school. When adults overly demand helpfulness, however (e.g., "you should help your parents with the dishes," "can't you see your little brother needs help?"etc.), it can be experienced as a burden, as something you do to please others or because you have to. Any personal satisfaction the young person might get from having contributed to the life of another is thereby erased.

In SBC young people get to notice times when they actually chose to help, why they did that, and the effects it had on themselves and others. Interestingly, young people also develop the skills to facilitate SBC themselves and start doing SBC, on their own, with their friends! Having the experience of being valued and supported through conversations, provides them with the intimate knowledge and skills to help and support others during hard times.

In sum, SBC enhances young people's ability to relate constructively to others in a variety of ways.

Table 2.3: Summary of effects on attitude towards others

	Skill Boosting Conversations focus on success	**Skill Teaching Conversations** focus on problem
Empathy and awareness of others' feelings	High, as young people are calm and receptive	Low, as young people are filled with their own emotions
Awareness of others' intentions and goals	High, as the positive emotions and safety embedded in the discussion make it possible to speculate	Low, as young people often assume the other intentionally wanted to cause problems and anger blocks other views
Awareness of others' context of life	Maximized	Minimized
Helpfulness toward others	High, as the person is more self-motivated and aware of the satisfaction experienced when helping their peers	Low, as helpfulness is experienced as a *"should"*; a smaller repertoire of skills is developed in relation to helping others

4. Effects on the adult-youth relationship

Distribution of power

One of the remarkable differences between talking to young people about problems vs. talking about successes has to do with the power relationship between an adult and young person (Freedman, Epston & Lobovits, 1997). In a problem-focused conversation (or even in a more neutral social skill training setting), the adult is usually trying to influence the young person to engage in or understand certain skills that the adult deems important. This exchange is, by its very nature, hierarchical.

When the conversation between adult and young person is centered on exploring a success, the relationship is more egalitarian and collaborative (White, 2007). The young person holds the knowledge, and all parties are intrigued and learning together in a reciprocal exchange (Zimmerman & Dickerson, 1996). This becomes particularly evident if this process is facilitated with a group of young people all contributing their hypotheses and ideas.

Connectedness and appreciation

Conversations about successes are exciting and tend to leave all participants feeling intimately connected and appreciative of the shared journey. In a traditional teaching conversations, that sense of connectedness and intimacy will vary greatly depending on the relationship with the adult.

Trust

In traditional teaching conversations, trust tends to be fairly fragile. In SBC, where successes and appreciations are woven into the very fabric of the exchange, trust is naturally enhanced.

Table 2.4: Summary of effects on the adult-child relationship

	Skill Boosting Conversations focus on success	**Skill Teaching Conversations** focus on problem
Distribution of power	More equal and collaborative	Hierarchical
Appreciation	Rich and bi-directional	Varies greatly depending on the way the adult is teaching
Connectedness	High	Varies greatly
Trust	High	Low to high

Questions and answers

Question. I can see how SBC can be very powerful on many levels, but don't you think that for some subjects, plain teaching can really have its place in getting kids to think more?

Answer. SBC apply mostly to skills of living and ability to think, not to academics (although most subjects *can* be taught in engaging and fun ways). Even if you are a teacher in a classroom setting, however, you will still have plenty of opportunities to use SBC, especially when teaching life skills.

Sometimes we are so busy trying to implant our own ideas in young people's brains that we forget to first look at what's already there. It can be helpful to remember that young people have an attention span about equivalent in minutes to their age in years when it comes to passively listening (Tileston, 2004). Teaching anything, then, often has to be done in small chunks in order to sustain the complete attention of the young person.

Question. I'm not sure about all of this. If people solved a problem once, can't they just solve it again with or without SBC?

Answer. I make a distinction between skills that are very situation specific and those that are repeatable. Consider the experience of, say, a man who was assaulted on the street and fought with all his might and successfully protected himself. Is this person in good shape to protect himself as well the next time? Not necessarily. He will most likely think he was lucky to get away and may even feel shaken and more vulnerable even though he was successful. Now imagine that I was to review with this person all the details of what he did well, how he kicked, punched, move around the assailant, slipped away, noticed his weaknesses, envisioned several potential escape and tricked him. Would he be in a better position to defend himself next time? Absolutely, especially if we justified, enriched, and connected his actions to his history of being an athlete and an emergency room physician.

Knowing exactly what he did well and why would transform his experience of the incident and his perception of his abilities in self-defense. He would be in a much better position to repeat the accomplishment if faced with this unfortunate situation again. Without such conversation however, he might be expected to react more from a place of fear and powerlessness and less able to protect himself if he were ever to face this situation again. SBC with people who have experienced trauma will be discussed further at a later time.

Question. SBC sounds fascinating but I don't fully get it. If kids are so good at thinking of helpful solutions, why in the world don't they simply just use them in the first place??

Answer. We tend to believe that behaviors are a reflection of people's thought process and intentions. Often, this is not the case either for adults or children. For example, how many women have the intentions of changing their eating patterns but don't actually do it? How many men want to be more involved and more patient with their children and fail over and over again? Motivation and the deep desire to do something is not always sufficient. We often need a little boost from someone supportive and an awareness of the tools we have with which to accomplish our goals.

It's the same thing for young people. In fact scientists used to believe that young people were doomed to be more directed by their emotions than their thoughts. Until recently, it was believed that they could not control their emotions very well because MRI studies showed that the amygdala, the center for fight-or-flight emotions, developed much earlier than the frontal cortex, which is responsible for impulse control (Papalia, Wendkos Olds & Duskin Feldman, 2008). Recently, some fascinating research has demonstrated that the brains of people involved in more reflective and contemplative processes displayed a brain development pattern different from that of the average American (for a review of the literature see Begley, 2007). Specifically, people who engaged in extensive daily meditation and conscious breathing had greater frontal lobe development than the average person. This exciting finding proves that we *can* reshape our brains through conscious mental activity.

CHAPTER 3

Defining Six Types of Successes

Even though successes occur all the time, actually noticing them can take a little practice for both adults and young people, especially here in the West. We are not encouraged to pay attention to our privileges and cultivate appreciation in our daily lives. For example, most people do not wake up every morning feeling grateful toward their bodies for the absence of ear infections. What would it be like to take one minute to notice all your body parts that are feeling good?! How would it change your daily outlook if you were to start the day every morning with an appreciative scan of your body (Kabat-Zinn, 2005)?

In general, in order to develop an appreciative awareness, people have to consciously pay attention to comfort and recognize successes. Since successes can only be recognized when we know what they actually look like, this chapter will give a detailed description and examples of six possible types of successes. Questions that can be used to discuss these successes with young people will also be provided.

Defining a success

A success is an experience of maintaining integrity and congruency with oneself in the face of a potential challenge. Successes exist in a wide variety of situations. For example, remaining calm when a situation is stressful or responding to another person's anger with empathy are both successes. A success often takes place when one's goals, desires, wishes, interests, needs, or experiences *could have* resulted in unpleasant experiences or conflicts *but didn't or did so in a controlled way*. The negative consequences were either prevented or limited in their scope.

Factors to consider in a success

For the purpose of SBC, readers may want to consider two main factors in identifying and recognizing successes:

1. *The process*: The experience of young people as they are facing the tricky situation. This refers mostly to their thoughts, emotions, and behaviors as they navigate the unexpected issue and attempt to determine how to respond. The complex internal activity involved occurs very quickly and is mostly invisible to observers. It can be organized into three general categories of responses:

   a. helpful ideas and attempts to solve the situation. For example: "This doesn't really matter to me but it looks important for my friend, so I'll let it go."

   b. unhelpful ideas/attempts that can worsen the problem. For example: "I'll get back at him later".

   c. a combination of both helpful and unhelpful ideas/attempts. For example: "This is so unfair, but I don't want to ruin the game for everyone else".

2. *The outcome*: The result of young people's attempts at solving a tricky situation. The outcome is what adults typically witness and can be organized into two

categories of responses: The problem was: a. solved or b. not solved. Partially solved problems are considered not solved.

Different types of successes

Combining the categories listed above, the three types of thoughts (Process) and two potential results (Outcomes) can be summarized into six possible successes (see figure 3.1):

1. the problem is solved and the process was constructive
2. the problem is solved and the temptation to do something unhelpful was contained
3. the problem is solved but the young person experienced both helpful and unhelpful ideas
4. the problem is not solved and helpful solutions were attempted but unsuccessfully
5. the problem is not solved, solutions were generated mentally but were not attempted
6. the problem is not solved and no constructive thoughts are remembered

As the reader may notice, adults tend to step in mainly for the unsolved problems. Completely unsolved problems (#5 and #6) are actually rather rare, and yet 90% of adults' interventions are focused on them. Granted, some problems need adult help and there are great ways of discussing these problems to mobilize an ability to change, such as with externalizing language (Beaudoin & Taylor, 2009; Freedman & Combs, 1996; White, 2007; Zimmerman & Dickerson, 1996). Externalizing will be introduced further in Chapter 8). The very point of this book however is that for the majority of young people, there are powerful ways of enhancing skills without talking about problems i.e. by focusing on their successes or attempted solutions.

Examining the six types of successes

Let's take a look at the six types of successes in action, using variations on one story of a conflict between two children. Remember, you don't need to memorize the six types. They are offered simply to provide you with a sense of what is possible. Once a person develops the habit of noticing hidden successes, he or she can become skilled at conducting SBC without ever remembering these particular categories. Also, while specific questions are listed for each type of success, I often use these questions in flexible ways. That is, the questions listed for category number one might just as easily apply in category number three.

1. The problem is solved and the process was constructive.

This is the hardest category of success to notice for both youths and adults. We rarely stop to appreciate interactions that are going well; we take them for granted. This is especially true if the problem is solved quickly.

This category of success includes both successes that are easily achieved and those that may have included the letting go of some small frustration. A success without any emotional charge is harder to notice than a success that included the presence of a small irritation.

Figure 3.1. Six different types of successes

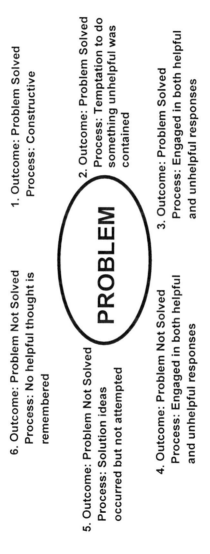

1. Outcome: Problem Solved
   Process: Constructive

2. Outcome: Problem Solved
   Process: Temptation to do
   something unhelpful was
   contained

3. Outcome: Problem Solved
   Process: Engaged in both helpful
   and unhelpful responses

4. Outcome: Problem Not Solved
   Process: Engaged in both helpful
   and unhelpful responses

5. Outcome: Problem Not Solved
   Process: Solution ideas
   occurred but not attempted

6. Outcome: Problem Not Solved
   Process: No helpful thought is
   remembered

PROBLEM

For example the first two lines of the dialogue below could have been considered a success without emotions for Miguel and would be easy to overlook. The actual event that unfolded however did end up including some minor irritation:

Miguel: Can I see the ball?
Emma: No.
Miguel: I just want to look at it for one minute.
Emma: NO!
Miguel: I'll look at it and give it right back!
Emma: NOOO! (and she leaves).
Miguel (shrugs with annoyance): Fine...

Entry into SBC
-*How question*: Inquire about the process by which he was able to maintain a constructive attitude. Example: "How were you able to not be too upset at your sister when she didn't want to show you the ball?"

-*Detail question*: Ask about the details of what you saw. "Were you surprised that she didn't want to show you the ball?" "Did you notice her eyes?" "Did your own body tense up?"

Caution
Sometimes when a success was really easy, young people may not give it much meaning. This category is particularly tricky because if you argue that this *is* a success when youths don't believe it is, you are forcing them to prove to you that it isn't! For example if you tell your child: "Thanks for giving your ice cream to your brother, that's really a success in sharing" and your child responds in an annoyed voice "No, I wasn't sharing, I just don't want it anymore," it is not worth it

to argue with "well, usually, even when you don't want your dessert you don't want to give anything to your brother." Such arguing has multiple negative effects: you disqualify the value of your observations, associate an unpleasant experience with SBC, and pressure the young person into a detailed description of how meaningless his behavior was. You are inadvertently reinforcing the "wrong" neural pathway! Remember, SBC is about honoring youths' knowledge and ideas about their *own* experience and putting ours in the backseat!

2. The problem is solved and the temptation to do something unhelpful was contained.

This category is one of the most powerful to explore as you have just about every useful element: successful outcome, successful process and on top of it all, a successful effort to contain unhelpful ideas! This type of success is almost begging for SBC! You can take the conversation in any direction but the most important one to explore would be how they contained unhelpful ideas.

> *Miguel: Can I see the ball?*
> *Emma: No.*
> *Miguel: I just want to look at it for one minute.*
> *Emma: NO!*
> *Miguel (leaning toward the ball and considering grabbing it): I'll look at it and give it right back!*
> *Emma: NOOO (and she takes off).*
> *Miguel (Shrugs): Fine.*

Entry into SBC

How question: Inquire about the process by which he was able to maintain a constructive attitude. Example: "How were you able to let go of wanting to look at the ball and just say 'fine'?"

Temptation question: Acknowledge the existence of a temptation and explore how the young person contained it. Example: "It would have been tempting for many people to try and grab the ball. What prevented you from doing that?"

Caution
The danger here is that sometimes we are more excited about the successes than youths are themselves. It is tempting to say with excitement:"Wow, do you realize that you almost grabbed the ball but you didn't? Amazing! How did you do that? That must have taken a lot of self-control." This is risky as the young person may be startled by your comment. They may become guarded or focused on *your* emotions, which will interfere with the genuine and introspective conversation about the event. Youths can't quietly go inward and reflect on themselves when someone is intensely emotional in front of them. In addition, it is hard for anyone, youths or adults, to identify our personal experience when someone is pressuring us to name it or itching to name it for us. The temptation is simply to reject what others are trying to impose without even giving the idea much consideration.

3. The problem is solved but the young person engaged in both helpful and unhelpful actions.

If you witness a conflict between two young people, you will most likely hear crappy arguments and some statements that will make your ears cringe. This is so difficult for adults to bear that many will intervene right away. In reality, there is a lot of evidence that left on their own, most young people will eventually find a reasonable solution to their issue (Faber &

Mazlish, 2004). This is often hard to believe in light of what we hear, but it is definitely valid and worth trying. Much of the work then becomes a personal effort: how much can you tolerate, what is your limit, can you give them a chance to experiment with problem solving, making mistakes and learning from their experiment?

Some parents need to force themselves to hold off by not intervening for a set five minutes. Others give each child five sentences after which they intervene. Of course this is heavily dependent on the situation. If you see a young person physically aggressed or about to be hit, then intervening immediately would be warranted. But how often is the situation so serious that blood or physical harm would ensue? With regards to words, many young people do not say or hear insults the way we adults do. For many these are just words. Make sure you pay attention to the effects of the argument *on* each child. Are they really being hurt by what is said or are they just upset by the overall conflict?

Miguel: I just want to look at it for one minute.
Emma: NOOOO...
Miguel(trying to take the ball from her hands and repeating):
I'll look at it and give it right back!
Emma: NOOOOOOOOO. (Screaming grabs the ball and runs).
Miguel (shrugs with annoyance): Fine...

Entry into SBC
Ending question: In this type of success you can inquire about the ending since it is successful in spite of a mix of helpful and unhelpful behaviors. Example: "I noticed you folks

having an argument about the ball earlier. What helped you end the conflict?"

Size question: This question brings attention to the magnitude of the conflict. Example: "You both wanted the ball earlier and I noticed it remained a small argument. How did you keep it small as opposed to having it turn into a big fight?"

Caution:
Since our adult view is often limited, we may occasionally assume a situation has ended when it hasn't. Ask Miguel the question above and he might say: "Well, we didn't solve it because I still want to see it." You can then inquire about what allows him to do something else in the meantime, or what enables him to wait patiently, and trust that he'll have another opportunity. Even if the interaction is not completely resolved, it is on hold and that in itself is a success.

4. The problem is not solved and the young person engaged in both helpful and unhelpful actions.

Similarly to the previous category, it is important for adults to wait, if possible, before intervening. When you think about it, this type of interaction will sooner or later become a type three category of success. All problems are eventually solved in some way or another: you either find something to do about it, you accept what happened or you move on and put it in the back of your head.

Miguel: I just want to look at it for one minute.
Emma: NOOOO.
Miguel (trying to take the ball from her hands and repeating): I'll look at it and give it right back.

Emma: NOOOOOOOO. (Screaming grabs the ball and runs).
Miguel (angry): Next time I'll know not to lend you any of my things, you stupid baby.

Entry into SBC
Double question: This helpful question makes it possible for young people to acknowledge their effort and state what they wish they had done differently. Example: "Can you tell me what you did that worked and what you did that may not have been so helpful after all?" The very awareness of having done something unhelpful and putting words to why it was unhelpful is a step in and of itself. Very often the reasons the young person will give you are completely different from what you were thinking. That's fine. Your goal is for them to notice the helpful and unhelpful aspects of their behaviors, not to see it your way.

Advice question: This question works really well when youths are ashamed or uncomfortable about discussing their behaviors. It moves the conversation away from them and focuses on imaginary "others" (Freedman & Combs, 2002). Example: "If this situation were to happen to your best friend, what advice would you give him on how to deal with it? How would you support him in letting go of the ball?"

Caution
The double question works well only in a non-punitive environment and trusting relationship. However, a derogatory tone of voice or language would not yield any thought-provoking conversation. An example of a negative version of this question would be: "Tell me what you did well and what you did that was really stupid." Young people must trust that

they will not be lectured if they acknowledge a mistake or express the wish that they had done things differently. They are making themselves vulnerable and willing to reflect on an error, which no one likes to do. It would be counterproductive to make them feel bad, guilty, or further ashamed about it. It is better to just listen and comfort. In fact whenever youths experience intense uncomfortable emotions, it is usually more productive to comfort and support them before engaging in SBC. In some situations, especially if uncomfortable emotions are manageable, SBC in and of itself may be calming. Paying attention to the effects of the conversation will ultimately tell you whether to pursue or not.

5. The problem is not solved, solutions occurred mentally but were not attempted. Only unhelpful behaviors were visible.

In this scenario, adults can be so busy doing conflict management that they overlook the helpful ideas that occurred mentally. This is particularly true if the conflict resolution with the two (or more) youths took a lot of time and energy. It becomes tempting to just move on and be done with it. It is especially important in these situations to draw out and pay attention to solutions that were imagined but not tried, as these were generated during an episode of uncomfortable emotions. Given that it is very hard for everyone, adult and youths, to generate constructive thoughts during intense uncomfortable emotions, the few helpful ideas that did come up reflect a potential alternative way of responding that can become more readily accessible to the young person and easier to replicate in the future. In other words, uncomfortable emotions can consume so much of our brain activity that if any neural pathways are already there firing alternative reactions, they are a real gem to recognize and build on.

Miguel: Can I look at the ball?
Emma: NO.
Miguel (tries to take the ball from her hands)
Emma: NOOOOOOOO. (Screaming, tries to run).
Miguel (grabs her angrily): Give me that ball.
Emma screams and kicks furiously, fighting to hold on to her ball.

Entry into SBC
Other part question: When any of us engage in destructive behaviors, there is almost always another part of us protesting our choice. In our example above, we could ask: "Was there a part of you that wanted to do something different?" "Did you hesitate a little before trying to grab the ball? If yes, what made you hesitate?"

Percentage question: This type of question invites youths to quantify the incongruence they experienced with their action. This is a helpful question even in serious situations such as with suicidal teenagers. When asked what percentage of the time you want to cut yourself, the answer is, usually less than 60%, leaving a big part of *him or her* already standing mentally against the decision. In the example with Miguel, it would be interesting to ask him: "What percentage of you wanted to grab the ball? What percentage of you didn't want you to do that?"

Caution
Again, the timing of SBC is particularly important in this category. Since the goal of SBC is to stimulate an experience of agency and competency, think carefully about the best time to ask your questions because you often won't be given an opportunity to talk about the same event twice. Most young people like to live in the present and they may not always be

excited about being drawn back into what seems like a past and unpleasant event, even if it just happened today or yesterday.

Since we are now in the categories where young people may experience a sense of failure or fear your criticism, careful consideration must be taken before talking. It is often better to wait a few hours for the dust to settle. You can also let them know gently that you want to chat about the event and ask them when would be a good time.

6. The problem is not solved and no helpful solution seems to have been generated or attempted.

To an observer, this category of interaction can look identical to the previous one. The main difference is that during SBC, the youth seems unable to remember having had any constructive thought. This does not mean that constructive thoughts were not there.

Miguel: Can I look at the ball?
Emma: NO.
Miguel (trying to take the ball from her hands).
Emma: NOOOOOOOOO. (Screaming grabs the ball and runs).
Miguel (angry and tries to catch her): Give me that ball.

The inability to recall using constructive thinking can occur for three clusters of reasons related to those involved: youth-related, adult-related, or context-related.

Youth-related obstacles to remembering their own constructive thinking arise from:
- everything happened so quickly that it was difficult to notice any thoughts at all (issue of speed)

- anger being so overwhelming that they cannot retrieve any other memories (issue of intensity)
- having developed such a negative view of oneself that it is too painful or discouraging to reflect back on the incident or oneself (issue of suffering)

Adult-related obstacles to youth remembering their constructive thinking can arise from:
- lack of relationship
- failure to establish safety and trust prior to engaging in the conversation
- tentativeness with regards to doing something new like SBC questions

Context-related obstacles to remembering constructive thinking include:
- poor choice of place for the conversation
- timing too close to or too far from the event
- unpredictable interference, such as phone ringing, sibling arriving, etc.

Context-related obstacles often arise because adults didn't set up SBC at a time and place that could lead to productive outcomes or didn't anticipate problems with the environment.

Entry into SBC

Exploring the worst questions: When helpful thoughts about an event cannot be remembered, it is always possible to explore what the young person didn't do that could have been worse (Jenkins, 1990). This type of question can go in several directions including: imagining the worst at an earlier *time* in the sequence of events or at a moment where it could have escalated to more *serious* behaviors. For example: "Miguel, why did you ask for the ball in the first place instead of just grabbing it right there and then?" "Why didn't you just kick the ball from her hands when she said no"?

The answers you will get are invariably a reflection of youths' values and preferences with regards to avoiding or minimizing conflict, the very ideas we want to support (White, 2000).

The moving on question: When the uncomfortable emotions have subsided and the young person seems to have found some inner peace, it is always helpful to ask how she or he was able to let go of the frustration in the end. For example: "It looks like you are feeling so much better than you were a few hours ago. How were you able to get over that frustration so quickly?"

The timing of this question in particular makes a big difference on the outcome. Asking this question early on may be met by an annoyed "I don't know," but if you ask this question later, it can have a completely different effect. When the young person has moved on and found some inner peace, she can tell you how she did it and what she told herself. And this awareness of thought, in the end, is the skill boost we are looking for.

Caution
As always, your relationship with the young person is what matters most. A young person deserves support even if he or she has engaged in the most despicable behavior. I should say *especially* if he or she engaged in a despicable behavior...since that is when any individual is most in need of a caring, growth promoting environment. You cannot effectively fight a habit of

oppression, for example, with additional oppression (Jenkins, 1990). Only an experience of compassion can provide a foundation for change.

With kindness, validation of each person's feelings, and gentle questions, you can open space for youths to understand each other. This is done without taking sides and seeking the right and wrong. If possible, each child can be given a chance to share his perspective in a context free of threats of punishment and other coercive method. Otherwise young people only want to defend themselves, prove the other wrong and become pinned against each other further as enemies. Our goal should be to accompany them through the process of expressing themselves, support the inquiry and generate helpful ideas.

Extra tip: Youths do not like to talk about unsolved events. I often give them the control by negotiating how many questions I will be allowed to ask and being playful in protesting the limit. This reverses the position of power or at least balances it. If it is really embarrassing to talk about this, it may be helpful to talk side by side, in a car, or at bedtime. Those contexts allow youths to avoid the discomfort of eye contact. In the most challenging situations, you can even lighten the conversation once in a while with a casual, out-of-context comment about the place you are in, such as "that was a nice bird just there."

General words of caution

With practice you will start noticing a lot more successes than you can talk about and that's very exciting! You can observe the unfolding of interactions and simply decide whether you want to comment on one just now or wait until later for more quiet, introspective discussion. A main consideration in this decision is the effect it will have on the youth. Will she be annoyed by having to stop what she's doing or postpone an upcoming fun activity because of your interest in a discussion? In such a situation you would be inadvertently punishing the child for having had a success. Some successes can just be acknowledged without needing further conversation. For example: "I really appreciate that you were patient there with the delay in our drawing project." The acknowledgment in itself has a positive effect even if awareness is not fully articulated.

Other successes can simply go un-discussed, remaining as positive memories. Those memories are not "wasted" as they were lived by the young person *and* will have an effect on your appreciation or patience with the child. SBC provide tools for supporting young people's experience of competency, but it does not mean you should watch young people's every actions and comment on everything. This would make them uncomfortable and have negative effects both on youths and your relationship to them.

Precious discoveries shared intimately during a SBC should never be rehashed during an unpleasant situation, a conflict, or even simply as an attempt to motivate the young person to do better. Even just one instance of doing this could be experienced as a betrayal of trust and understandably impede youths' willingness to engage in SBC with you for a long time. The tools shared during SBC belong to youths, and *they* will determine when and how they are able to use them.

A skill boosting conversation is a private, intimate moment to cherish. It stands on its own and should not be used against young people in any conflict, ever. For example, shouting "I thought you preferred to be a calm person…well, you sure have a long way to go to get there…" will NOT be helpful.

In sum, the following is a short list of what *not* to do:

- Constantly evaluate young people's every action in a way that makes them uncomfortable
- Bring up successes too often to the point where the young person is exasperated by your desire to talk
- Attempt to do a SBC at the "wrong" time when they're excited about something else or busy
- Remind young people of the constructive things they said in a way that implies expectation or criticism
- Use the intimate knowledge shared during SBC against the young person as a put down during a conflict

Questions and Answers

Question. I'm really curious… Is Miguel's story true, and if yes, did you decide to have a conversation with him or did you let that one pass?

Answer. The story in category one was the true story of Miguel. All the others were modified versions to explain the different possibilities of success. I did have a delightful conversation with Miguel right there and then because he was left there standing alone and a bit grumpy. So I approached him, tried to engage him, and he was responsive. Should he have been unwilling to talk about it after a couple of attempts or further aggravated by my questions, I would have stopped right away. Here is a reconstruction of our SB conversation:

MN: Hey, I'm impressed at how you handled the beginning of this...

Miguel (no answer, still grumpy).

MN: It looks to me like you are having some frustration right now, but you were being very patient there. Would you say that too or would you call it something else?

Miguel: I don't know.

MN: I think it would have been hard for a lot of people to do that. Were you telling yourself something that helped you try a solution?

Miguel: I'm not sure.

MN: I wonder for instance if not wanting to share something at a certain time has ever happened to you?

Miguel: Yeah, sometimes I just want to finish playing with something.

MN: Could that have been what was happening to Emma just now?

Miguel: Yeah, I guess (his face relaxes).

MN: Is that a part of what you may have been paying attention to?

Miguel: Well, I could tell she really didn't want to hand the ball to me.

MN: When you could tell she didn't want to hand it over, did you have an understanding of why she was like that?

Miguel: Well, she was probably afraid I would take it from her because I do do that sometimes...(awareness of his contribution).

MN: So, you remembered you take her things sometimes so it made sense she didn't want to share? (nods) So you understood her position. Does understanding another person's position help solve things?

Miguel: Yeah, I guess it helps.

MN: In understanding her experience it sounds like you also were able to remember past incidents that contributed to her reactions…those past incidents were sort of invisible but still having an effect?

Miguel: Yeah, I guess I was able to understand her and remember past things.

MN: Yeah, and you did all of that while controlling your own upset feelings! What do you think of yourself doing that?!

Miguel: (smiles shyly but pleased).

MN: What would have happened if you had tried to grab it?

Miguel: She would have yelled, we would have fought, and I would have gotten in trouble.

MN: She would have yelled, you would have fought, and there would have been trouble. Would that have affected your day afterwards?

Miguel: Yeah, I would have been grumpy.

MN: Yeah, and then you'd have people mad at you?

Miguel: Yeah, that's true…

MN: Instead everyone has stayed sort of okay?

Miguel: (amused) Yeah!

MN: Had you thought about that too?

Miguel: Not then, but I did kind of want to avoid a fight.

MN: Ah, so you wanted to avoid a fight? (nods)

Miguel: I was having a good time playing my game and it wasn't worth it to get into a fight about that.

MN: So you wanted to keep your good time. Is that a little like thinking about the consequence? (nods) That could be hard to think of the consequences on our good time in a situation like that. Does that mean you reminded yourself that the ball was not so important?

Miguel: Yeah, it's less important than having fun.
MN: Ah, so you kept in mind what was most important in this and let go of the rest? (nods). You did a lot of things in your head to keep peace! (smiles). What are you most proud of having done?
Miguel: I guess I'm glad I kind of understood why she didn't want to share.
MN: What makes you glad about that particular idea?
Miguel: Well, I think it really did help me not grab it from her.
MN: Would you say you were "being understanding"?
Miguel (blushing a little): Yeah, I guess!
MN: Did you know you could be an understanding person?
Miguel: No!
MN: What is that like to discover?
Miguel: It's kind of cool!

Question. These ideas are so interesting, but I don't think I could use them because I'm just too busy and I don't see enough to observe or talk about these moments of successes.

Answer. This is not a problem. It simply puts you in the same position as counselors and therapists who have to use specific strategies to uncover hidden successes. This is a beautiful art, based in neuroscience, and we will explore it right now in chapter 4.

CHAPTER 4

Looking for Treasures

Successes occur all the time. It is simply impossible, however, for any observer to see all the successes of anyone, youth or adult, because we do not see the thinking inside their brain and because we do witness all of their activities. Probing young people to identify and share successes that occurred in our absence can be very fruitful and exciting. It is like looking for a treasure. You know there's probably something there, but you need special tools to find it. I will be introducing just such tools in this chapter.

You may wonder, why bother with successes you haven't witnessed? Well, if memories define who we are, then it becomes critical to help young people remember the best of who they can be in various contexts, and this doesn't always happen in front of us. What goes in and out of our memory is important because, as Mark Van Doren writes, "memory is the companion, the tutor and the library with which we travel" (cited in Ellis, 2007, p.97). If you care about young people, helping them build a rich mental library of recognized skills, strategies and successes that occurred in different contexts can be a great gift to their socio-emotional intelligence. Another way to think about it is that you are providing them with great tools, like a really good first aid kit or Swiss army knife for their journey through life!

Discovering these unnoticed treasures requires artful questioning, because young people often forget "minor" incidents or do not recognize a success as a success. In this chapter, we will look at three types of unnoticed successes:

1. forgotten
2. unrecognized
3. witnessed

Advances in neuroscience and studies of memory have given us important information about how to best extract *forgotten* successes. *Unrecognized* successes require a different set of digging tools, because what caused them to be forgotten is that the problem was resolved without uncomfortable emotion; that is, it never occurred to the person that she or he was solving a problem. Finally, we often *witness* successes in the lives of others but don't pay close attention to what happened. It can be enormously useful to draw a child's attention to how friends and peers at school resolve conflicts or problems.

I will now review the process of discovering these three types of unnoticed successes.

Forgotten successes

Engaging a young person in a detailed conversation about an event that we haven't witnessed can seem challenging. In reality, it isn't that difficult most of the time and there can be several advantages to this process. In particular, we are more likely to see the event through the young person's eyes and ask about details in a way that we might not have done if we had seen the event ourselves. In addition, since the young person knows we weren't there, she or he may be more willing to comment on little details and be patient with our questions;

when we ask a lot of questions about events we did witness, young people can more easily become bored or annoyed.

Since young people may not remember the events you want to call forth, such SBC rely heavily on a few fascinating aspects of memory and its processing.

How memory works

Much of people's memory processing occurs between the frontal lobes and a brain structure called the hypocampus. Interestingly, encoding (or committing to memory) seems to involve the left part of the frontal lobe while remembering or calling up the memory activates more the right hemisphere (Tulving, 2002). This is believed to explain why people look to the left when remembering autobiographical memories since left side movements activate the right prefrontal regions (Siegel, 1999). The hypocampus, on the other hand, is a tiny bundle in the middle of the brain that would fit in the palm of your hand, and yet it encodes everything you experience. Experience consists of information provided by all the senses (sight, touch, smell, taste, sound), mood, meaning, context, thoughts about the event and connection to other similar experiences.

"Memory is more than just what we consciously recall" (LeDoux, 2002, p.133). The brain encodes a lot more than what we pay attention to. This is demonstrated by fascinating empirical studies where, for example, a subject is given a pair of headphones and instructed to only pay attention to the list of animal names played in their right ear and ignore the list of flower names played in their left ear (Bentin, Kutas, & Hillyard, 1995). When participants are asked what they heard in their left ear, they usually don't know. However, when they are asked to fill in the missing letters in a list of flower names, they outperform subjects not exposed to the flower list at all. This means that the information was encoded in their brains, but they cannot access it *at will* because they didn't pay attention to it at the time it was being encoded. It is, however, retrievable when someone provides them with the appropriate memory cues.

If we were to consciously notice all of the information that goes into our brains, we would be overwhelmed and unable to function. To protect our brains from being surcharged with useless information, much of daily life experience is encoded unconsciously and then later on erased from awareness *unless* we actively attend to it or call upon the memory.

This "use it or lose it" aspect of memory means that unless *unnoticed-successes* are discovered, discussed and consolidated, most will be forgotten within a week or so. This is not to say that we should be probing our children's brains all the time but rather it's an invitation to pay attention, and to ask questions, especially when we know there is a good likelihood that something special happened, as we will see in the example below.

The extensive information encoded by the brain is stored as a web of interconnected neurons that fire together. One of the classic pillars of neuroscience is that: "neurons that fire together, wire together" (Hebb, 1949). Once you find one thread of the web, you can slowly and progressively unravel a lot of the remaining parts. For SBC, this means that you can enter the web of information through any of the more easily accessible units of information, and progressively make your way to what the young person thought, felt, and experienced during any particular event.

Entry points into the memory of forgotten successes

1. Mood and uncomfortable emotions

Transitions in moods and emotions are a good indicator that young people faced a tricky situation and that some form of thinking probably happened (White & Epston, 1990). More specifically, transitions into uncomfortable emotions indicate a problem-solving event, and transitions out of uncomfortable emotions represent an ability to recover from the incident. Both of these often involve successes. For SBC purposes, asking young people about changes in their mood or emotions during the day provides an easy entry into successes. The following questions can be used:

- Was there a time today when you felt things weren't great? What was happening?
- What was the hardest part of the day?
- Any time when you felt annoyed by one of us or by someone at school?
- Was there a time today when you could have been upset but you weren't?

There are other types of emotion descriptors that are also helpful to notice such as intensity and frequency (Ekman, 2007). Intensity refers to the amplitude of the emotion, how big it was. Frequency refers to how often it happens. People's progress away from problems is often at first visible by a reduced intensity and frequency of uncomfortable moods and emotions. This reduction indicates more successful problem solving and also, feeling better about oneself, being more tolerant of others and making better decisions.

Emotions are among the most powerful scaffolds of memories. Some authors have even proposed that the strength of a memory depends on its degree of emotional activation (McGaugh, 1992; LeDoux, 2002). This idea was first proposed well over 100 years ago by theorists such as William James who even suggested that emotions, especially intense ones, can almost be understood as leaving "cerebral scars" in the brain tissue in the form of "lasting changes in synaptic connectivity" (cited in Siegel, 1999). Helping kids identify the skills they used to handle various emotionally charged experiences throughout their day can have a powerful impact on how these events will be remembered and the quality of the "cerebral scar." Moreover it can lead progressively to a brain structure that is rich with positive emotions about oneself and one's socio-emotional competency.

2. Senses

One of the fastest and most primary ways information reaches our brain is through our senses, even when we are not aware of it (Restak, 2007). Young people in particular, can be much more connected to their senses than adults are. By using questions that help recall sensorial memory, adults can bring young people back to the time and place where the event took place. This may require using a series of questions to recreate the details of the experience progressively. In other words, you want to use questions that tap into various sensory memories:

- Were there a lot of people over there? (sight)
- Were there any nice smelling flowers? (smell)
- Were the chairs really cold to sit on, it's been so cold lately! (tactile)

- Did you eat your yummy snack? What did you eat first? (taste)
- Were there a lot of birds in that park. Could you hear them singing? (auditory)
- Were your legs all sore from that running or could you still move? (kinesthetic)

For example, if as a parent you were told that an issue had arisen between your child and his friend in the park, you could ask: "How was it at the park today? Was it windy? Did you play a lot on the play structure and climbed everywhere?" As an educator or counselor if you were informed of an incident in the cafeteria, you can always attempt to re-trigger youth's memory by asking: "What were they serving at the cafeteria today? Was it good? Did the smell fill up the air? Were most of the students eating pizza or bagels?"

Some young people have a stunning kinesthetic memory. For this reason, schools using cutting-edge research even recruit this type of memory to learn academic material. For example, a fun spelling exercise for first graders is to have them hop as they say each letter of a word, placing their legs open or closed depending on whether the letter is a vowel or a consonant. They find that kids are much more likely to remember these spellings than those learned without the kinesthetic exercise.

3. Context

Many authors have discussed the use of contextual clues as strategies to trigger the recall of information (Ellis, 2007; Schacter, 2002). Context, the environment in which an event takes place, can provide a rich entry into SBC because it includes so much information. It also allows for the conversation to start with the big picture surrounding the event, and then narrow it down to the recollection of a few precious sentences recorded in a person's brain. I often like to ask young people to help me picture the scene. In doing so, I recruit their own mental imagery into an active process of regenerating the context.

Exploration of context includes the general event descriptors: who, what, where, when, and how of any incident. The question "why" is usually avoided at this stage to avoid shutting down the recollection flow. It involves a different brain process. Questions about context include:

- Where were you exactly?
- Who was there?
- Was that this afternoon?
- What were you folks doing? What were you talking about?
- How was it? Were you having fun?

With context you can recreate a vivid memory of the experience and watch as the youth goes right back to the place, time, and event. Once the child is back in the event, it becomes easier to progressively scaffold a conversation toward his or her thoughts, feelings, and the meaning of the success.

Remembering the context in which an interaction took place not only enhances the retrieval of a memory but also its future recall. Research has shown that when instructed to visualize the imagery of a story, students were later on much more likely to remember details. This is particularly true for 4th graders and above as compared to lower grade students (Schneider, 2004).

This may be because sequential memory develops fairly slowly and doesn't really click in until about the age of 9 or 10.

Example

Here is a private conversation that I had with an elementary school boy, Ronaldo, who had claimed that, unlike his classmates, he didn't really have any successes. Since I knew this boy as kind and thoughtful, I was convinced that I could extract a success somewhere somehow, using my knowledge of memory, emotions, senses, and context.

MN: You don't think you have any successes? Let's check that out. I'm pretty sure you do. Can you remember a time in the last week when you might have gotten upset with your friends?
R: No, I usually don't get upset.
MN: So how about at recess. What do you like to do at recess?
R: I like to play soccer.
MN: Who do you play with?
R: I play with Nick, Antonio, and Tom.
MN: Do all three of you always want to do the same thing?
R: Yeah, most of the time.
MN: When was the last time you didn't want to do the same thing?
R: Well, yesterday I wanted to play wall ball for a change and they didn't want to.
MN: Where were you exactly?
R: We were on the big field.
MN: On the big field by the tree and play structure?
R: No, by the water fountain and the fence.
MN: It was so hot yesterday. Were you getting a sip of water?

R: Yeah, we were. It was really hot.

MN: So I'm imagining you by the water fountain with your three friends after having taken a sip of water and being hot. You told your friends about wall ball. How did they react?

R: Well, Tom said he didn't want to run anymore, he wanted to play the wizard game, and Nick and Antonio didn't really care so much but were more tempted by the wizard game too.

MN: What did you do?

R: I tried convincing them a little, and then I thought to just go play with the others at wall ball, but then I thought it might hurt my friends' feelings so I just stayed with them.

MN: Was there a part of you that could have gotten frustrated?

R: Yeah, because it's the third time in a row that I wanted to play wall ball and they didn't.

MN: What did the frustration want you to do?

R (shy): I felt like saying a bad word but I didn't. I thought, it's so hot, I'll just go along with them today, but I told them that tomorrow I was going to do wall ball even if they didn't want to.

MN: Did "letting them do their thing" work out for you and your friends?

R: Yeah, cause I let them know ahead of time and it didn't hurt their feelings.

MN: So is it possible that this could be a success? Instead of saying a bad word when there was this disagreement, you took into account your friends' feeling, played their game one more time, and let them know ahead of time that it was going to be important for you to play wall ball the next day?

R (smiling): I guess!

The simple process of reactivating memories of interactions with his friends allowed us to find situations where differences of opinion had to be negotiated, leading to successful problem solving.

Unrecognized Successes

As we saw earlier, in chapter 3, young people, like adults, do not readily notice the *absence* of problems. They tend not to give themselves pats on the back for something well done. For example, a young person can have made spectacular progress at getting along with a peer at school and yet when asked, did you have any success today, reply genuinely: "no, not really." This type of unrecognized success refers to those situations where the young person handled a challenge without a trace of uncomfortable emotion. The young person employed skills of socio-emotional intelligence so successfully, with such acceptance, peace of mind, and constructive actions, that his memory of it is as a "non-issue." It simply doesn't come up on the radar if asked to name a recent success. For these unrecognized successes, which are vitally important to uncover, it is especially helpful to have some knowledge of the activities in the young person's life and to be able to guess where problems (and successful problem solving) could have occurred.

Also, when you know a young person well enough, whether you are her parent, teacher or therapist, you can fairly easily provide a description of her personal problem triggers. For example, if you know that students in your child's class always fight over who's out at wall-ball, then you know that's an area to inquire about, once in a while. When you are aware of the particularities of a problem, you are in a better position to notice its absence.

These types of questions use exactly the same who, what, where, when, and how described above in the context section but in a very different way. Take a minute to think of one of your children and answer the following questions:

- What is the hardest situation for this child?
- Where is the problem most likely to occur?
- With whom is the problem most likely to occur?
- When is the problem most likely to occur?
- How does he usually get himself in trouble…?

If you are able to answer these questions, then you have points of entry into conversations about successes. For example, say Jenna hates losing a game, particularly when playing with Sophie at the school's morning recess. When looking for a success, you can take a minute at the end of the day to ask Jenna if she played with Sophie and then progress from, "what did you folks do" and "where," to, "did you have fun" or "did everything go well? I know you've been having some hard moments lately." You may be surprised at what good SBC you are able to do.

Example

I had just such an opportunity with my son when he was in third grade. His class at school had taken a pioneer walk field trip that day. The kids had all dressed up in pioneer clothes, eaten pioneer food, and teams of five children were asked to pull a wagon up and down very steep hills on a ranch! I knew the goal of the day was also to allow children to do teamwork and solve their own conflicts, and that the adults were just there to ensure safety. Here's a recap of the conversation we had after he'd shared his excitement about the day with me for a good 20 minutes:

> *MN: So, did you have a success at solving anything tricky with your teammates?*
> *M: No, I didn't.*
> *MN (surprised): Really? You folks all worked hard together and had no conflicts?*
> *M: No, really, we didn't have any problems.*
> *MN: Was there a time when you could have been even slightly annoyed or tired of someone?*
> *M: Nope.*
> *MN: I wonder how you avoided conflicts. In a situation like that it's so easy to think that one person isn't working hard enough or feel like someone isn't doing his part.*
> *M: No, we didn't fight over that because I simply did most of the work.*
> *MN: You did?!*
> *M: Yes, I'm the one who pulled the wagon most of the way because the others couldn't.*
> *MN (curious without judgment): And that was okay with you?*
> *M: It was okay with me but it was really hard work and I got really tired.*
> *MN: What is it that helped you be okay with that especially when you were tired?*
> *M: Well, Simon just came out of his cast and I thought it would probably not be good for his recovering broken arm to push a wagon up a hill, and then Pat never does any sport so he was always just wanting to lie down. I thought just walking the trail was hard for him. Elizabeth's not used to walking either and she looked so miserable that I didn't dare ask her, and then Anna, well, we had put her in charge of*

shaking the butter so her hands were busy. In the end, for me it wasn't so hard because I'm used to hiking so what was hard for them was a bit easier for me, so then it was okay!
MN: What does it take for someone to be able to do that and be okay with it?
M: I don't know ... understanding how people are different ... maybe?
MN: So you were being "understanding of differences"? (nods) Do you like being a person who understands how people are different? (nods).

As you can see, it would have been very easy to miss this success because he wasn't considering it one. And yet, he was using all kinds of skills such as perspective, compassion, and relativity that were well worth extracting and noticing. With a teenager I might have continued the conversation to explicitly name with him the variety of skills involved. However with my tired son, that particular day, it was enough talking!

Witnessed Successes in Other Peoples' Lives

Like adults, young people see the world through their brains. What we encourage them to notice has a great impact on their future perceptions of themselves, others, and life in general. Exposure to just about any social interaction or problem-solving situation is an opportunity for them to view, support, and appreciate competency.

This is especially true when young people witness the success of a friend or family member and comment on it. So many of these moments happen throughout the course of a day or week that it's best to single out only the significant ones. Depending on the young person, their age and gender, you may not be able to engage them in SBC much more than once or twice a week. Make your choices wisely. You can also use stories from your own personal life, books, plays, TV, and the general witnessing of people in the park or in stores, etc.

Discussing successes of parents, family and friends

When using your own experience as a parent or educator, you can acknowledge times when you could have gotten angry and chose not to. A good example of that is when driving! It is a fruitful opportunity to share the temptation to be angry versus to model compassion. You can ask youth why they think the other driver is behaving this way and share your own hypothesis. It can even be a game: maybe the other driver is a doctor needing to go to an emergency or a very tired person not paying attention very well. You are boosting the skills of compassion and a multiplicity of perspectives to explain a person's behavior as opposed to always narrowly thinking that the other is annoying.

A most powerful way of using SBC with regards to the lives of other is to encourage youth to notice the successes of their friends and other family members.

Noticing other people's successes allows your child to learn vicariously, i.e., young people learn a great deal by watching the social and emotional experience of another and how they deal with situations (Papalia, Wendkos-Olds & Duskin-Feldman, 2009). Research has also shown that young people raised in environments where their own and others' various experiences are discussed seem more interested in and able to understand other people's emotions in general (Bretherton,

1993). And in so doing they learn how important it is to self-reflect and discuss what's going on in their minds.

Discussing successes in the media

It can be great practice, and important to a young person's development, to also look at the successes of people they don't know. Books, plays, and TV shows for example, provide an endless opportunity for SBC, especially since many children's authors put suspense in their book by having youth lie in dangerous situations or by completely villainizing another person, a sibling or a parent. When my kids read books I like to raise questions about whether people can really be all "bad" and all "good" or if most people are a mix.

This less personal practice of SBC, where we are not talking about our children's lives but still asking them to think about social reality, allows young people to develop their analytical skills and expand their awareness of the bigger perspective of life. Once again we must not overdo it or we risk ruining a powerful possibility for growth.

The true art of uncovering

The reconstruction of a memory is profoundly affected by which questions are asked, the experience of young people retelling their story, their emotions at that very moment, and their perception of the listener (Siegel, 1999). Uncovering the memory of a success, is an art that entails thoughtfulness, presence and involved listening. Just as you would concentrate and move slowly to scaffold a castle of cards, uncovering private experience requires progression in small increments, sometimes asking a minute-by-minute description of what happened (see Figure 4.1). Using the youth's language (Zimmerman & Dickerson, 1996) also prevents interference with the precious unfolding of the memory. In other words, using your own adult language runs the risk of interrupting the inward movie-like experience of young people and propels them outward to ask you what a word means or to tell you that you didn't exactly understand what they meant.

Retrieving the memory of an event requires using a cue that will be significant enough to trigger recollection (Sousa, 2006). The more we know about exactly how children encode information, the better we are at re-eliciting the event. Young children for example tend to remember particular details of an event better than older youth, who tend to remember only the gist (Reyna & Brainerd, 1995; Brainerd & Reyna, 2004). More specifically, kindergartners may remember someone's shoe color or one salient word a speaker used, while older youth would remember the general message in a speech but not the verbatim. This has to do with the development of their brains and age-related differences in information processing ability.

Also, while this may seem obvious, young people will be better able to comment on the implications of successes if you are able to trigger the memory of the event *in its original sequence,* that is, what happened at the very onset, in the middle and how it generally unfolded. Since people tend to have an easier time remembering the beginning and end of a sequence, you'll often have to do more mining work in order to retrieve the middle section (Sousa, 2006).

The art of uncovering also requires you to make decisions about whether or not to pursue SBC, postpone the process, or change conversational directions.

Figure 4.1: Mining for successes

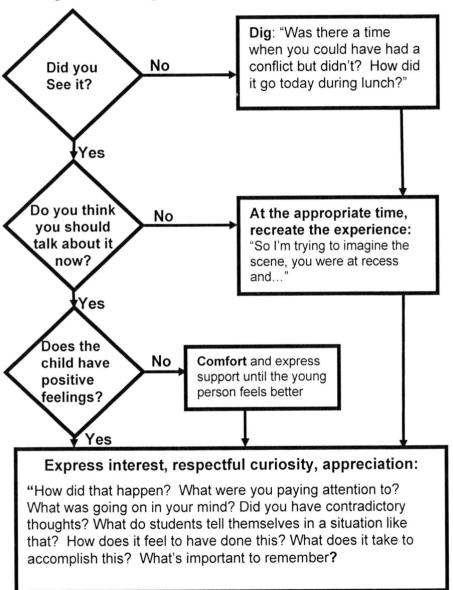

Questions and answers

Question. So, could we say that just asking questions about a success in and of itself will make a difference, or does it matter specifically what kind of question we ask?

Answer. The kind of question does matter to some extent. Research shows that parents who ask "elaborative" types of questions foster a greater ability in their children to talk for longer periods of time and share more details (Cleveland & Reese, 2005). The three-year-olds in these families even remember events better several years later (Reese, Haden, & Fivush, 1993)! Elaborative conversations involve supporting and expanding on the discussion in a way that is mutually rewarding for the adult and the young person. This is in contrast to "repetitive" style of conversations where parents seem to be "checking" what the child remembers. These are experienced more like an interrogation.

Question. You mentioned that emotions are really important in shaping and encoding memories. Is the young person's emotion while you are talking about successes important?

Answer. Absolutely! Memories are not like videos that remain the same regardless of the number of time you play them (Sousa, 2006). Every time you activate a memory, you change it. It becomes relearned and enriched by your interest in it or the different perspectives on it. You strengthen the neural pathway of some of its parts and attach the present time experience to it. So if a young person becomes profoundly annoyed at retelling the success, that feeling may be added to the story. If the young person becomes proud, then the story gains emotional power in the brain. In other words, the act of retriggering a memory allows it to be stored again in a modified form. Retrieval is a "memory modifier" (Bjork, 1989). Each retrieval increases the ease and likelihood that it can be retrieved again.

Question. My preschooler never seems to remember anything when I ask him questions about his playdates in the park. Could I use some of these brain retrieval strategies with him to find some successes or is he just too young?

Answer. Generally speaking, mining for these treasures is only successful in children older than four or five, because of the limited development of the medial temporal lobe (which includes the hypocampus) and the frontal cortex before that age. The maturation of both of these brain areas is necessary for children to develop a sense of time, self-knowing, and sequencing of events (Siegel, 1999). The development of autobiographical memory in and of itself is also linked to the acquisition of language skills (Nelson, 2005) since an event has to be encoded with words to be able to be retrieved by words later on (Reeder, Martin & Turner, 2010). This late development of the autobiographical and episodic memory leaves very young children hampered in their ability to independently retell the story of what happened to them in time unless the event is enacted *and* objects are used. Specifically, if a story is pretend-acted *and* relevant objects are handled at the same time, the memories of these children will better recall the story (Haden, Ornstein, Ekerman & Didow, 2001).

For SBC purposes, this means that a four-year-old boy could be engaged in the retelling of his success, being kind but assertive with his friend grabbing his sand toy at the park, if his guardian *and* he retell the story by acting it *and* using the sand toy in their demonstration. This process of co-acting and handling will also bridge the child's limited vocabulary and his greater understanding ability (Hollister-Sandberg & Spritz, 2010).

Question. This stuff is exciting. My daughter's teacher told me she did an amazing job at solving a conflict today! If I manage to get the conversation started, what do I do then? How do I go about moving deeper into SBC?

Answer. The first SB conversation is always exciting and challenging. You know there is so much you can do and are often sitting on the edge of your seat trying to remember how to tap into all the possible areas! Go slowly and don't forget to stay with the young person's content and experience. In our next chapter we will discuss many different ways of pursuing SBC. You can choose a way that seems most comfortable for you at this time and experiment with others later on. The goal is to help young people grow beyond the success and further develop their actual skill so that it becomes a repeatable problem-solving knowledge.

CHAPTER 5

Legos and Skills

You have found some successes and are ready to move on! The next step is to realize that each small detail of information about an event is like a building block or a piece of lego. You can leave the blocks scattered on the "floor" of the mind, build a cage with them by focusing on the problematic aspects of the event, or use them to progressively assemble a museum of valuable treasures.

Leaving them scattered is like ignoring the event and not seeing any value in these blocks. They will eventually be brushed aside or put away in a closet somewhere. A cage is built with comments such as, "You're so impatient, why can't you wait a minute longer" when the child has already been waiting for a long time. A museum is built with acknowledgments such as, "I know you've been waiting for a long time already and you're getting tired. Thanks for having been so patient, I'll try my best to finish this really soon." The event is the same, the building blocks are the same. The difference lies in which blocks you seek and choose to see, and how you decide to use them.

This chapter is about getting more details and examining the implications of every useful aspect of successes. Building blocks for emotional skills will be discussed first, followed by those for social skills.

Emotional skills legos

From infancy, young people face the challenge of dealing with complex emotions often with very little knowledge and tools. If raised in a nurturing environment, they will learn some of these skills from their caregivers or be comforted in ways that will later be internalized (Siegel & Hartzell, 2004). In many situations, however, young people can feel quite overwhelmed, frightened, and powerless in dealing with what's happening inside. In our BAFTTA school counseling program, one child even asked if we could please change his brain because he really didn't want to be angry and in trouble all the time but just couldn't help it.

In SBC related to individual problematic emotions, I attempt to highlight two particular aspects of experience:

- personal agency (they are capable of dealing with the emotion)
- taking action (they have concrete ways of dealing constructively with the situation).

Personal agency

Whatever the emotion, it is important to make young people feel confident in their ability to handle what's happening. If young people are regularly exposed to SBC, this sense of agency can develop fairly quickly since they realize that they are able to come up with solutions themselves. It is most helpful if the valuable ideas generated become credited to both the creativity of young people *and* the conversational process. This ensures that young people will feel competent to handle their emotional life themselves and to continue to seek support when dealing with a hardship.

If SBC focus on the part of the brain that contradicts the uncomfortable emotion, useful ideas will be generated. Indeed, no one ever tolerates suffering passively (White, 2004). Since our brain is always firing a complex set of ideas, you can always ask "is there another part of you that thinks differently about this?" As we saw in chapter 3, even the suicidal teenager will recognize that a part of him or her doesn't want to die. Acknowledging the coexistence of these thoughts automatically provides experiences of choice.

The reasoning coming from young people's own set of counter arguments can be more powerful than any logical argument you can make as an adult. The goal of SBC then becomes to bring to the forefront the helpful part of the brain that usually functions quietly in the background of awareness and to shrink the presence of the uncomfortable emotion. The simple act of asking the young person to talk and articulate the helpful part activates the firing of those neurons and automatically reduces the power of the unpleasant emotion.

This is well illustrated by an interaction I had with my son when he was 8 years old. He had become fearful after reading Harry Potter with his friends and woke me up in the middle of the night after having a nightmare:

Mike: I'm so scared, I just can't sleep anymore…
MN: What is the fear telling you?
Mike: It's telling me that I'm like Harry Potter except I have no magical powers and Voldemort is hiding somewhere waiting to harm me.
MN: The fear makes you think Voldemort is hiding to harm you? Is there a part of you that thinks something different than that?

Mike (much thinking): I guess there's a part of me that thinks that Voldemort has no reason to harm me specifically because I have no magical powers. He harms only wizards and I know for sure that I'm not because I never did any magic, not even by accident.

MN: So remembering that he harms only wizards and that you're not a wizard is helpful. What other arguments do you have to shrink the fear?

Mike (pausing and thinking): I guess it doesn't make sense that he's hiding, why would he do that? He'd have no reason to wait until later to harm me.

MN (interested): So, thinking that he has no reasons to wait. What else can you tell the fear?

Mike: Well, I don't have magical powers but there are things that I could use to defend myself.

MN: So you have tools to defend yourself? Like what?

Mike: I have my rocks from my collection that I can throw and my Native American stick.

MN: True, so you can defend yourself with these objects. Anything else?

Mike: I'm not sure…

MN: Does the fear make you think that Voldemort is real?

Mike: Yeah, that's true, it does that, but now that I think about it he's not, he's been invented by someone.

MN: Does that make a difference--remembering that he's been invented?

Mike: Yeah, it helps me not imagine all these things. I can remember it's all in my imagination and not for real.

MN: Okay, so Fear tells you 1. Voldemort is real; 2. He wants to harm you; 3. You're like Harry Potter but with no power. And you're able to reply to the Fear that 1. Voldemort was invented by someone; 2. If he existed he'd

*have no reason to harm you; 3.You have objects to defend
yourself with.*
Mike (smiling and relaxing): Yeah!
MN: So how is the fear now?
Mike: Much smaller!
MN: Can we go back to sleep now!
Mike: Yes!

This example makes visible how it would have been delicate
for any adult to argue logically against the fear. Many children's
fears appear irrational to our adult minds so we are not in a
good position to tackle them from the outside. Only the mind
that generated the fear can generate the most powerful counter
arguments against it. In other words, only the mind that
generates the poison can generate the perfect antidote.

With Mike's nightmare, the fear came from within and so
did the solution. This left my son with tools to face his own
imaginative world and encouraged his sense of competency in
dealing with intense emotions. He knows that even if he's on
his own, he can always ask himself if there's another part of his
brain that thinks differently.

Taking Action

Research has shown that people tolerate challenging
emotions much better when they have a specific action that they
can take (Anderman & Wolters, 2006). For example, heart rate,
blood pressure and cortisol production are much higher when
people experience or witness suffering without being able to
take actions. This is well documented for example, in events
involving natural disaster and giving people the possibility of
making donations (Ekman, 2007). While most people, young
and old, will find ways of coping with their experiences, some

strategies work better than other. Helping young people notice the methods of coping that work best for them equips them with important skills (Henderson & Dweck, 1990). Left to their own trial-and-error process, young people may feel more helpless than is necessary or develop ways of coping that have negative effects.

For example, as I am writing this book, one of the doctoral interns I supervise in our school counseling program is working with a young boy, Andrew, who recently lost his beloved cat, Trickle. The grief has been so overwhelming for Andrew that he has started mimicking cat behaviors to maintain the presence of Trickle in his life. While many cat-ways could be socially acceptable, Andrew, unfortunately has taken on the habit of licking his hands when they are dirty. At school, this behavior is met with reactions of disgust from both teachers and fellow students.

The idea of keeping something of his cat alive in his life is a quite clever way of dealing with grief. "Licking" however, may not be the best cat behavior to take on, because of its social effects. SBC with Andrew then become a process of helping him recognize the cleverness of the idea and bringing forth *other* ways of keeping the cat in his life, such as being affectionate, kind, a fast runner, or quiet. If they are discussed early on, before he becomes too stigmatized in school, issues such as these can be readjusted very quickly with SBC.

Social skills legos

Successes found in social interactions involve a more complex set of variables to explore, since another human being is involved. When discussing social successes with youth, it is most valuable to explore the following four areas of skills:

- thinking just before the success
- consideration of self during the success
- consideration of others during the success
- the rippling effects of their choice

As an example, take the story of Terry, who successfully resisted the temptation to insult Jana, who was cheating in a game. Instead, she decided to just leave the game saying, "I don't want to do this anymore":

- her thinking before the success was "I really don't like her but I shouldn't say mean things".
- her consideration of herself was "I'd rather just go play with someone else who's more fun".
- her consideration of Jana was "she's annoying but it's kind of sad she doesn't have any friends.
- the rippling effects after the success included more fun, less conflicts, no trouble, and feeling better about herself as a person that she didn't unnecessarily hurt Jana.

The airplane metaphor

As illustrated in figure 5.1, most children and many adults more easily remember the four categories described above by visualizing them as the major components of an airplane:

- the airplane nose represents the starting point of the successful response and the initial thinking that steered action in a helpful direction. This initial goal is usually to keep the problem small.

- the two wings of the airplane represent the dual consideration of self and others.
- and the tail of the airplane represents the positive rippling effects or valuable "luggage" that are brought into the future as a result of the constructive choice.

Figure 5.1 The airplane metaphor

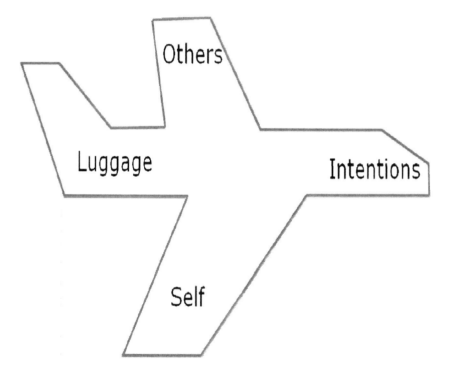

If one or more pieces is/are missing, the plane may have trouble successfully navigating through the weather of challenging social interactions. When all complex "parts" of an airplane are assembled or when people consider these four areas in their problem solving, they become able to "fly" over tricky situations as opposed to "crashing" into them. In the next section, we will look at the application of these four categories of inquiry in a conversation with a teenager.

Example: Adam and the poetry reading

The four categories of inquiry are illustrated in the following transcript of a conversation I had with one of my clients, Adam.

Adam is an athletic teenager, seriously involved in the development of his professional soccer career. He is telling me about a success he had when he found himself unexpectedly stuck with his mother and older sister who were driving to an amateur poetry reading an hour away from their home. The initial plan had been to drop him off at a friend's house on the way, so that he could enjoy a pleasant evening of sports. Because of a miscommunication, no one was at his friend's house when they arrived...

I will now explore his thinking before the success, his consideration of himself and others, and the rippling effects of his choice. Although his mother is in the room with us, most of the dialogue transcribed here is between Adam and me.

Thinking just before

This category of inquiry refers to what goes on in young people's mind just as they are confronted by the tricky situation. Thinking just before responding to the situation is critical as in a fraction of second a single thought can steer the unfolding of the situation in a constructive or intensely destructive direction. These initial thoughts are highly dependent on a person's repertoire of emotional, cognitive, behavioral, and experiential responses. Until people are made aware of their presence, most do not experience these thoughts as choices but are simply flooded with a jumble of experiences (Beaudoin, 2005). An absence of awareness leaves young people vulnerable to simply reacting based on the baggage they are carrying in their brain, i.e., what they've witnessed, lived, experienced.

With SBC extracting the components of successes, young people develop a heightened awareness of the menu of helpful possibilities generated by their frontal cortex even in its most subtle forms. They also deeply reinforce the neural pathways of these responses, making them more readily available next time. With Adam, I was intrigued by his initial thinking about unexpectedly having to go to the poetry reading and how he steered his experience into a constructive direction.

MN: What was happening for you when you realized you wouldn't be able to stay at your friend's house on the way and had to go to the poetry reading?
A: I was really disgruntled.
MN: What was happening in your mind?
A: I was expecting a fun evening with my friend, playing soccer, watching TV, listening to music, and instead I'm stuck sitting in a car heading for an evening of poetry reading. Not only that, it got worst. At first, I thought the poetry reading was only one hour long and then I found out it was three hours long. I was really angry. And, on top of it all, halfway there I realized my mom brought only veggies because my sister is vegetarian. It was a horrible feeling.

MN: So you were stuck in the car, had only veggies, and realized that you would be at the poetry reading for a long time. You were disgruntled. What were you tempted to do?
A: I really felt like picking a fight, but my Mom reminded me that if life hands you lemons, you make lemonade.
MN: Did you agree with her?
A: Yeah, I sort of did, I believe that, too.
MN: When you had that thought that you needed to make lemonade, what did you decide to do?
A: I don't think I decided to do anything.
MN: So I'm imagining you in the car. Are you looking out the window? (nods) You're really disgruntled, and your mom reminds you about making lemonade. How did that affect what you did right after that, given that you agreed with her?
A: Hum...I don't know...I think that ... after a moment, I just decided to hide that I didn't want to be there.
MN: You decided to hide that you didn't want to be there?
A: Yeah, I didn't want my negative mood to carry over to things. You know, how when you're in a bad mood, everything you come in contact with is tinged negatively. I couldn't be in a good mood so I did the best I could to at least be in an "undecided mood" and keep an open mind in case something good could come up.

Adam's initial choice of being in an "undecided mood and keeping an open mind" set the stage for the unfolding of the success. It was valuable for him to put words to this initial thinking, perhaps for the first time, so that it becomes a clearer option the next time he is faced with an unpleasant situation. This is particularly important because that helpful thinking was generated *during* an uncomfortable emotion. Helpful thoughts that come up during an uncomfortable emotion have the potential to create a powerful anti-problem neural pathway for the young person. The conversational process reinforced the neural pathway for this thought and made Adam more aware of this mental tool so that he can choose to use it again later. To recap, Adam's thinking process became accessible with key questions such as:

- when you realized you wouldn't be able to stay at your friend's house, what was your first thought?
- when it occurred to you that your mother couldn't follow the plan, what came to your mind?
- what happens in people's mind when they are suddenly struck by a situation like that?

Consideration of self

Consideration of self refers to one's awareness of the complex set of personal needs, feelings, desires, intentions and hopes that may influence our actions. This is illustrated in the second part of my conversation with Adam:

MN: So you decided that you didn't want your negative mood to tinge everything. You wanted to be in an undecided mood and keep an open mind in case something good happened. Concretely, how did you make that happen for yourself? Sometimes it's hard to switch our mood.
A: At first, I just stayed silent for some time.
MN: What did you do during the silence to move away from the anger and take care of yourself?
A: I tried to listen to music to get a little happier.
MN: Is that something you know about yourself, if you listen to music, it makes things better?
A: Yeah, it always does.

MN: Then what did you do that was helpful?
A: I'm not sure, I think just listening to music helped.
MN: Just listening to music helped. You know sometimes when I listen to music my mind wanders and makes me think of things. Does that happen to you? (Nods) Could that have happened then when you were in the car and heading to the poetry reading?
A: Well, for sure, I tried to imagine how it would feel when it would be over.
MN: Imagining the end? How did you imagine the end?
A: Just the relief of coming back home and finally being able to do things I like.
MN: So listening to music and thinking of the end helped during the drive down there. How about during the poetry reading, how did you take care of yourself then?
A: During the reading I was really falling asleep and since it was a small room my sister kept on elbowing me every time my head would lean so that I wouldn't offend the poets.
MN (laughing): She wouldn't let you sleep? How did you occupy your mind to not fall asleep then?
A: I didn't want to offend the poets even though some of them were soooo boring and would go on forever... they were supposed to read only one piece but a few of them disregarded that rule.
MN: What do you do when you're so bored and have to sit awake somewhere for a few hours?
A: The only thing I could come up with was to remember fun conversations with my friends. I did that for a while and eventually I started counting how many flowers were left in the bowl (every poet was given a flower after their reading).
MN: So remembering fun conversations and counting the flowers.

Adam took care of himself and maintained his choice of action by remaining silent for some time, listening to music, thinking about the end, remembering fun conversations, and counting the flowers.

Consideration of self works well when it is balanced with a consideration of others, otherwise the person may act in self-centered ways. Note however that many youth are self-centered for a long time and that it is a natural part of development (Santrok, 2009). Through kind conversations this awareness can be gently activated, but too much pressure will backfire at adolescence. I have worked with a few teenage girls who had been systematically pressured, too early in their development, to focus on others and not be "so selfish." When their brains naturally led them to be more aware of others, they became overly pleasing, self-conscious, and unable to say no to any of their friends' requests. The pendulum swung the other way and led to dangerous implications. Excessive adult pressure of any kind on developing youth often backfires.

In sum, with Adam, consideration of self thinking became accessible with key questions such as:
- what was important for you to do when this happened?
- what was happening inside of you that made you feel a little better?
- how did you take care of yourself?

Consideration of others

Consideration of others refers to young people seeing the other player as a person rather than just as an annoying object. It involves noticing the other person's needs, feelings, desires, intentions, hopes, and requires the mental ability of perspective taking. It usually develops between the ages of 6 and 8 (Hollister-Sandberg & Spritz, 2010). Consideration of others is a step away from the narrow self-centeredness that often clutters conflict resolution. In part three of my conversation with Adam, I was wondering if thinking of the other people involved had occurred and been helpful.

MN: I'm imagining you in the car, driving to this poetry reading, and trying to keep an undecided mood and open mind. You're listening to music to make you a little happier and then start thinking of how it will be when the evening is over. During the reading you thought of fun conversations and counted the flowers. All of those strategies helped you move away from the disgruntled angry feeling. Might there also have been any thoughts about your mom or sister that were helpful in moving to that place of open mind?
A: Yeah, well, I did realize early on that my anger could hurt all of us, myself, my mom and sister ... and the poets...
MN: You realized your anger could hurt all of you?
A: Yeah, I could have been whining, picking fights with my sister, and driving her up the wall. I could have let everyone know how much I disliked being there, but I chose not to.
MN: Was there any thought in particular that made you choose not to?
A: I'm not sure...Well, I guess...I guess I knew how important this poetry reading was for them and I didn't want to spoil it for them.
MN: So you thought of how important this poetry reading was for them. Would you say you cared about them even though there was the disgruntled feeling?
A: Yeah, plus it wasn't really their fault if I was stuck going with them.

Considering others can sometimes soften young people's experience and assist them in containing their anger. This is especially the case when the people involved in the unexpected event typically enjoy a caring relationship with each other.

To recap, Adam was able to access "consideration-of-other" thinking with key questions such as:

- Could you understand why she/he felt that way?
- Can you imagine what would make someone react like this?
- Did any thoughts cross your mind about the other people there?
- Was there anything helpful to consider about others?

Rippling effects

Rippling effects are the natural consequences of successes (White, 2007). In general, the word "consequence" must be used with caution because it can trigger a negative and punitive association for many youth. I prefer to call them implications, effects, what happens after, results, etc. More than with any other category, exploring the rippling effects makes visible the positive effects of youth's successes and choices. It helps them realize, *often for the first time*, that their helpful thinking made great things possible and allowed them to avoid really unpleasant experiences. This process has significant impact on their feelings about the event and consequently on their memory of the helpful thinking itself.

This is illustrated in part four of my conversation with Adam:

MN: So, you thought of how important this poetry reading was for them and you didn't want to spoil it for them. Does that mean that you were aware of the effects the anger could have? Or that you thought of the different directions this situation could go?

A: Well, I knew that if I did pick a fight, my sister would be mad at me for a couple of weeks, and then I realized it would be even more horrible if we argued throughout.

MN: So, you realized it would be more horrible if you went with the anger part of you not only during the evening but also for a few weeks after?

A: Yeah, I guess in some ways.

MN: Did that increase your motivation to stay in that undecided mood and keep an open mind in case something good happened? (Nods) Did anything good happen in the end?

A: Yeah, at some point I left to explore the building and its surrounding, and I eventually discovered a beautiful soccer field. I really enjoyed seeing it!

MN: Really? What was beautiful about it?

A: It was overlooking all of Monterey and had a beautiful view. I'd love to play in a field like that someday.

MN: So, you got something out of the experience after all?

A: Yeah, that soccer field is memorable.

MN: What effect did it have on you to realize you actually did shift your mood from disgruntled and angry to an open mind?

A: Well, I'm proud that I made it through the end.

MN (to Adam's mother): What effects did it have on you that Adam was able to do this?

Mother: I really appreciated that he did that. It gave me a warm and fuzzy feeling toward him. He's big and mature now!

MN: He can make lemonade!
(Everyone laughs)

The conversation ends with a discussion on the meaning of this success and the kind of person Adam is choosing to become.

Awareness of rippling effects has a direct impact on the sense of power and competency of young people. As illustrated in this example, young people develop the ability to be the master of their experiences even in situations where they seemingly have very little power.

Rippling effects can be explored by two different sets of questions: First, questions making visible the direct implications of their success; second, questions highlighting the escalation of problems they avoided by responding to the situation in a constructive way. These questions can target many areas of life such as: mood, thoughts about oneself, amount of fun, relationship with peers, parents, teachers and others, behaviors, activities, the rest of the day, etc. When SBC can make visible a series of rippling effects and summarize them, youth are often amazed and more than ever committed to using their strategies again. Such awareness of their skills paves the way for them to feel like a skill-ionaire!

Adam's airplane

Adam was able to metaphorically "fly an airplane" over the problem instead of having a miserable evening of conflicts. His "airplane of success" was built by his:

- initial decision to make lemonade and be in an "undecided mood, with an open mind" (airplane nose).
- considering his own experience by staying silent to not tinge everything negatively; listening to music to make himself happier and think of fun conversations with friends (one airplane wing).
- considering others by not wanting to spoil it for his mother and sister (the other airplane wing).
- awareness of the rippling effects of his choice such as avoiding a two-week conflict with his sister, not making it more horrible than it already was, and finding a beautiful field (airplane tail).

It is commonly believed by some that youth have little self-awareness and cannot think of consequences until much later in adolescence because the analytical and meta-thinking abilities required are assumed not to be available to them yet (Papalia, Wendkos Olds & Duskin Feldman, 2008). It is my experience however that even young brains can develop this ability if nurtured and encouraged to do so.

Questions and answers

Question. I read somewhere that the memory is more likely to encode events experienced with negative emotions than the ones with positive emotions. If that is true, how do you get youth to remember their successful problem-solving strategies in a lasting way?

Answer. It is true that memory is more prone to encoding intense frights, for example, than intense joys (LeDoux, 2002). We tend to ruminate a lot more on our dissatisfactions than our comfort. Some of that tendency comes from the necessity of remembering dangers if our species is to survive (Hanson & Mendius, 2009). SBC attempt to deal with this issue in two ways. First, by making conversations meaningful and connected with complex networks of values and memories already deeply set in the brain. Second, by having conversations about what young people avoided, ironically using the power of uncomfortable emotions to encode agency. Although more research would be needed in this area, helping young people recognize their avoidance of highly unpleasant experiences in and of itself can probably be assumed to trigger a part of the same encoding mechanism.

Question. Does this really work with younger children? I can't imagine exploring any of these categories with a child under the age of 7 or 8?

Answer. With younger children, the exploration is much simpler and may only require a couple of questions. Take this example with my daughter:

Amelia (calling out): Mommy, Mommy!
MN (unsure of what's happening but being clear it's not her emergency voice): What is it?
Amelia: Mommy, come!
MN: I'm in the middle of cooking dinner. Can you wait?
Amelia: Mommy, come, I need you.
MN: Okay, one minute, let me take this off the stove.
Amelia (no answer).
MN (walking to her and kneeling by her side): What is it? Are you okay?

Amelia (answers calmly): Well, now I'm okay, but I bit myself earlier and it was really, really painful; now it's almost gone.
MN: Really? What made the pain go away?
Amelia (thinking): I don't know, just waiting I think, ... but also I took a lot of big breaths, like this (demonstrating) and then I blew one really hard through my nose and I think I blew hard enough for the air to go out of my nose and into my mouth and blow on the booboo!
MN: So you made things better yourself? Time helped and deep breaths help! I'll try to remember that next time I bite myself!

In this example, Amelia was invited to notice that she had been able, on her own, to reduce her experience of pain. I also leveled the hierarchy of agency between us by letting her know that I would remember her trick next time I hurt myself. This elevated her knowledge and abilities since she not only helped herself but potentially her mother too!

Had she been unable to answer my initial question regarding how she had solved it, I would have simply wondered out loud and tried to guess, casually, some possible solutions she might have used.

As a matter of fact that happened later on that same day when we were leaving home in a rush and I realized I forgot a paper by the door. As I informed Amelia that I would run inside to grab the paper and come back in less than a minute, she started screaming and crying that she wanted to come with me. I firmly and gently said that given the late hour, I really couldn't take her out of her car seat just for a quick run back and forth. With tears in her eyes, and a flushed little face, she calmed down somewhat and reluctantly said, "okay." A second later, when I came back, she was still uneasy but calm and I asked her how she contained the fear. She had absolutely no idea even with the best of my questions. I then simply speculated out loud, *without* asking her to answer: "I wonder if you just told yourself, Mommy will be right be back, I know she will; or I've done it before and it was fine." Then I changed the subject to avoid overwhelming her and reversing the experience of competency.

Indeed, when a young person just doesn't know, asking too many questions that are all answered with "*I don't know*" can ironically create a sense of *incompetency*. It is important to leave the young person with a feeling of capability. I trusted that even if the strategy itself hadn't been identified, noticing the accomplishment of having calmed herself down would be a contribution to her burgeoning sense of emotional competency.

CHAPTER 6

Developing a Mental GPS

The repetitive process of experiencing SBC allows youth to develop not only a collection of concrete problem-solving skills, but also a conscious memory of their abilities to engage in different ways of processing information. In other words, while each SB conversation focuses on the content of a variety of specific events, the process in and of itself is always the same: inviting youth to notice their thinking *and* the big picture of the situation. Specifically, the activity of reviewing events in this particular way, over and over again in a developing brain progressively enhances neural pathways to examine life events with more awareness and a greater perspective.

The particular step discussed here, involves a shift from the *after the fact,* satisfying realization that one successfully navigated the solving of a tricky situation, as illustrated in the previous chapters, to making more deliberate and educated choices *during* the actual process of solving problems. In other words, young people regularly exposed to SBC can increasingly consider a broader range of information, which progressively gives them access to a wider menu of possible solutions. This new, expanded way of processing information allows people to solve a greater number of problems, more quickly, and can be applied to a wider variety of challenging situations. Successes no longer occur randomly but are generated through conscious awareness, analytical thinking and peace promoting choices. They are metaphorically acting as if they had a mental GPS!

Research has shown that when young people have expertise and practice in an area, they can even outperform adults in that particular specialty because the neural pathways in their brains are primed to notice and process this specific type of information. This was demonstrated by Ericsson and colleagues in 2006, and earlier on by Chi in 1978, who compared chess playing 5th graders and college students on their abilities to remember chess piece positions and sequencing. The children's memories and analysis of the actions were superior but *only* in chess playing. The neuroplasticity of children's brain is such that the repetition of enjoyable meaningful experiences creates a powerful canvas of pre-existing knowledge to which details can easily be attached and accessed later on.

Examples

Let's take a more in-depth look at youths' enhanced problem-solving reasoning using the stories below.

I finished my lunch before my friends so I told them that I would wait for them on our usual bench by the fence. So I waited and waited, distractedly watching the soccer game down the field. At some point, I realized that my friends were just having fun at the other end of the blacktop. Katy

My little brother was playing on my bed while I was doing my homework and then suddenly I realized that he had peed on MY pillow! Raoul

During an entire sleepover, my friend criticized my behaviors with my boyfriend and convinced me he was going to breakup with me the next day. I was so depressed that I avoided

him all morning until I realized he behaved as if nothing happened.   *Anna*

My sister lied to my Dad about needing the computer to do her homework. I knew she just wanted to watch her cheesy soap show but unfortunately they believed her and I had to get off from my sports highlights.   *Luis*

I was walking away from the field, proud that my two goals made us win the game, when I was knocked from behind by a powerful ball. I turned around with a yelp and saw Jonathan just standing there looking frustrated.   *Nikos*

I had worked really hard to sculpt a beautiful arrowhead in a small rock. I was really excited about it but just couldn't get the last edge polished right. Seeing my struggles, my friend offered to help with his tools but then within minutes...he broke it!   *Matt*

How would YOU respond to these situations?

For each of the above stories, take a minute to consider how it would feel to be in such a situation and what you would be inclined to do. Notice the emotions that would bubble up, the behaviors you would be tempted to engage in, and the words that might come out of your mouth... You can also imagine the response of a young person in your life.

How do you think skill-ionaire children would handle these events?

Skill-ionaire children and adolescents handle these situations slowly with awareness of their own experience (*meta-*

awareness), and a broader perspective of themselves, the situation and other people (*"invisibles"*).

Meta-awareness

With SBC young people are trained to develop meta-awareness by becoming increasingly aware of: 1. their own thoughts and feelings; and 2. the complex and often contradictory facets of these experiences. Specifically, awareness of their own thoughts and feelings involve the development of the ability to identify an experience *and* put words to it. This awareness develops progressively between the ages of 4 and 8 at which point a number of young people are able to notice that they are "thinking thoughts" (Flavell, Green & Flavell, 2000).

Awareness of complex and contradictory facets of experience involves a certain distancing from *and* examining of the content of our minds. Instead of experiencing confusion from these contradictions, young people are comfortable enough with the labeling of each individual experience to now distinguish and label them even if they are occurring at the same time. In other words, they can watch the contradictory thoughts and feelings in their minds as if they were metaphorically watching clouds glide through a blue sky (Kabat-Zinn, 2003). Since this awareness was developed in the context of examining successes, it is associated with a positive feeling and is devoid of the uneasiness that could otherwise derive from observing one's own destructive emotions. Young people become used to acknowledging the common presence of contradictory experiences and comfortable with discussing them metaphorically as parts of their brain.

In the first story of this chapter, Katy immediately experienced hurt, betrayal and anger when she saw her friends having fun without her in the distance. But she also quickly noticed that she was having those emotions, was able to name them and halt their negative impact by generating alternative understandings of the situation. Through SBC, she had determined that she valued being a flexible person and had been trained to examine a variety of hypotheses. On her own she started thinking:

- "I could think that they're not really my friends anymore but then maybe they were just sidetracked by someone who told them to come and see something"
- "I'm really unsettled by this, I can't let it go without checking it out with them"
- "Maybe they just forgot because it's been so long, it doesn't mean they don't like me"

In general, such awareness of oneself coupled with a big picture perspective opens the door to agency and an experience of choice. This awareness occurs on many levels and sublevels. Specifically, during an event, young people become able to:

- realize that they are having unpleasant emotions
- notice on time the temptation to engage in unhelpful actions
- become aware of the problematic implications associated with the temptation
- maintain control over their uncomfortable emotion and temptation to hurt
- generate or connect with more neutral or positive experiences of the situation

- stay connected to various possibilities of action
- choose an option that seems feasible, relevant and likely to succeed

On a broader meta-level, they become able to maintain a connection with their priorities, values and the kind of person they prefer to be.

Equipped with such an elaborate awareness, they become increasingly empowered to make decisions consciously. If experience is always multifaceted and you are aware of your preference for flexibility, then you know to search for your "flexible part" when responding to events. In other words, awareness allows you to further activate your own brain's firing for "flexibility" by anchoring yourself in its associated sensorial and experiential cues. Katy was able to remind herself that she valued being flexible, which was associated in her brain with a collection of memories of her successes at handling situations in a flexible way. As she walked towards her friends, she took a deep breath and trusted that everything would be okay and that she could handle this situation just as she had handled her earlier successes. It turned out that her friends were on their way to see her and had been sidetracked by someone's discovery of a ladybug gathering.

Meta-awareness or being aware of one's thinking is almost like watching yourself on a video and commenting: "I look pre-occupied; you can tell I was worried about grandma's health crisis. Oh! See I'm also able to smile and focus on Joey's silly behavior." In SBC, young people are invited to watch their brains and notice their different experiences. This observer's position unavoidably leads to a certain distance from the emotional experience and limits its intensity and escalation.

Meta-awareness activates the middle prefrontal cortex which allows it to slow down the reactive process (Cahn & Polish, 2006). This experience is similar to what occurs in basic mindfulness trainings where people are taught to notice their own thoughts without reacting.

Big picture understanding and "invisibles"

Young people develop big picture understanding by being encouraged to put themselves in others' shoes and infer what I call "invisibles." The "invisibles" are the important factors that influence people's behaviors. Someone's "invisibles" may include being hungry, having had a bad day, being worried about a karate test, being sick, having forgotten their lunch, etc… They include all the factors that may inadvertently render a person more prone to certain behaviors and emotions. "Invisibles" are not seen by the naked eye. We only become aware of them by analyzing the factors pushing people to engage in a given response. "Invisibles" are based in the belief that there are always complex reasons why people do what they do.

In SBC, young people are continually encouraged to ponder on what may have led the other person to engage in her behavior. Questions such: "How do you understand this person's actions? Is there anything you know about this person, that explains what she did? What's the big picture of life of this person? Is there anything about this person that helps you be patient with her?" Research shows that children as young as kindergarteners have some awareness that a peer, for example, on the other side of a board, may see things differently than they do. At level one of perspective taking, they will be able to verbally instruct this peer as to how to build a tower of blocs just like theirs (Flavell, 2004). But they will sometimes forget that this peer cannot see and may fail at correctly inferring what can and cannot be seen.

By seven and eight years old, children reach a level two of perspective taking and are more accurate in inferring another's view. This is also visible in studies examining children's thought process when they want to cheat in a game. Children at a level 1 in perspective taking will only pay attention to whether or not the adult can *see* them. Children at a level 2 in perspective taking will try to predict how the adult might actually think, and may more readily engage, when taking a test in school for example, in distracting the teacher or using a deceptive technique such as feigning to drop their pencil when they are in reality looking at their neighbor's answer in a test.

In addition to this developmental age difference, the abilities to put oneself in others' shoes, understand them *and* infer what may contribute to their experience seem to be affected by gender and cultural variations. Girls seem to mature earlier than boys with regards to perspective taking. Some theorists argue that this is the result of social trainings where girls are more encouraged than boys to focus on others and take on empathic roles (Tannen, 1990) while others believe that it is associated with different patterns of brain maturation (Kahil, 2005; Gurian 2001). As for the cultural difference, collectivistic countries have been found to place greater emphasis on social cohesion and parents encourage their children to avoid affecting others with anger while individualistic cultures encourage their children to express themselves (Shiraev & Levy, 2007).

While all these variations definitely need to be taken into account, I have found that young people of both genders, older than four years old, can generally use one or more of five types of "invisibles" if they have experienced a number of SBC. These "invisibles" revolve around: personal, relational, situational, contextual, and historical information.

Personal "invisibles"

Personal "invisibles" refers to the intrinsic ability of a protagonist to engage or not in a certain choice of action. For example, in the second anecdote above Raoul first felt a surge of frustration and a temptation to push his little brother off his bed. Almost simultaneously however, his mind flashed his brother's "invisibles" and he was able to think: "he's still a little kid and hasn't fully developed the ability to control his pee yet...." Raoul just called his mom for help and eventually felt sorry for his little brother who was himself horrified and tearful about his accident.

Relational "invisibles"

Relational "invisibles" refer to the shared past experience of people who have known each other for some time. In Anna's story, she was able to realize that her friend not only had never had a boyfriend throughout middle and high school but also that she was intensely envious of Anna's relationship. This awareness triggered some compassion and allowed Anna to let go of her frustration while still acknowledging that she would be more cautious before listening to her friend's dating advices!

Contextual "invisibles"

Contextual "invisibles" refers to what is happening in the current life of a person, such as what occurred earlier that day, the status of family relationships, socio-economic status, the general happiness and health of the person, etc. When Luis let his older sister on the family computer, he at first felt frustrated and resentful. Pretty quickly however he calmed down because he knew all too well that she was unhappy since her boyfriend had left her and that this show provided her with a relaxing distraction.

Historical "invisibles"

Historical "invisibles" refer to what has happened in the distant past, such as trauma, losses, accidents, etc. In the soccer game story, Nikos turned around in surprise and frustration and then noticed Jonathan's resentful look. It brought back memories of Jonathan's white and grey face when he was treated for leukemia a few years ago in 4th grade. He was bald and missed a lot of school. Jonathan had never caught up with the rest of the students in term of sports' ability and had increasingly developed bad sportsmanship manners now that they were in middle school. Nikos decided that he just wanted to focus on his joy from his own performance and walk away. Anyway, he thought, in all those years it was the first time Jonathan ever did something to him and then maybe, it was just an accident. He chose to let it go.

Situational "invisibles"

Situational "invisibles" refer to particularities of the specific circumstance at hand, such as facing an unrealistic task, confusing directions or a strong likelihood that an object will break. In story five, Matt's first reaction was one of anger. A part of his brain internally shouted: "YOU broke my arrowhead"! At the same time however, another part of his brain was able to consider many different types of "invisibles": "He didn't mean to, he's my best friend and he was just trying to help. Anyway, I might have been the one breaking it if I had continued what I was doing because it was really fragile and we didn't have the right tool."

Implications of seeing "invisibles"

Considering "invisibles" increases the likelihood of more accurately resolving problematic situations. Paying attention to "invisibles" increases youth's general ability to experience empathy and compassion because it widens their understanding of people beyond the boundaries of the here-and-now incident. In many interactions, in fact, "invisibles" have an even greater influence on someone's response than the limited visible aspects of incidents themselves. For this reason, the process of acknowledging "invisibles" is particularly powerful because seeing the big picture naturally reduces the emotional roller coaster by depersonalizing events, i.e., problems are no longer ascribed to intentions alone.

The process of acknowledging "invisibles" is also powerful because there are always more solutions to problems in a big picture understanding than in the narrow view of an event.

When young people see more of the problem in the context, they see more of the peer in the person.

Combining meta-awareness and big picture thinking

The skills of meta-awareness and big picture thinking allow young people to choose what they will be focusing on. This selective attention is needed all the time in schools. For example, young people need to be paying attention to their teachers while a friend may be goofing around and another may be secretly eating a candy. In such situations most students will, by age 5, know where they are supposed to focus their attention but may not necessarily be able to do it or know how to avoid being distracted (Berger, 2009). When dealing with social and emotional situations, many young people do not know neither what they should be paying attention to, or what to do about it, which leaves them vulnerable to just reacting. SBC contributes to creating their very own mental program, or GPS, specifying what is helpful to notice *and* what are possible responses afterwards.

Another way of thinking about this process is to imagine a person stuck trying to figure out their own emotional experience. In such a situation, there is not much space for anything else than gut reactions. When you've developed the ability to be aware of yourself, others, and everyone's "invisibles," you are suddenly faced with quite a landscape from which to find empathy and solutions. You can see the inadvertent contribution of each person (including yourself) and the complex ramification of contexts. You can also recognize commonalties, i.e. that you might react this way as well if it were you. Being able to put oneself in another person's shoes, even though you are in conflict with that person, often triggers some empathy and is associated with better peer relationships, especially in elementary schools (LeMare & Rubin, 1987). This awareness of others may also allow for feelings of love, friendship, care, or appreciation to coexist with the frustration of the conflict. In many ways, this combination of skills can be understood as reflecting *intra*personal skills and *inter*personal skills (Gardner, 1983, 1993). The implications of these skills will be discussed more extensively in the following chapter. I will now illustrate the process of extracting meta-awareness and "invisibles" with an example.

Helping young people actually see "invisibles"
The broken Barbie doll

As mentioned earlier, our memory retains and encodes a lot more information than what we actually attend to. In this interview, you will see me bring into Karen's awareness unattended details about her friend and progressively heighten her ability to notice others when she's upset. As you will see, her brain had taken a snapshot or a mental photograph of her friend and her "invisibles" but she hadn't consciously considered these factors when she responded to the event. Since she successfully solved the event, talking about it provides a golden opportunity to extract these unattended observations and bring them in the forefront of her awareness, hence reinforcing the neural pathway to do this again in another situation.

MN: You wanted to share a success at not getting upset?
Karen: Yes, a few days ago, my friend broke my Barbie doll and I didn't scream at her even though I really wanted to.
MN: She broke your Barbie doll and you managed not to scream. So I'm trying to picture the two of you; were you at school? How did she break your doll?
Karen: Yeah, we were at school by the play structure. We were playing with my Barbie and then at some point she wanted to bend her legs so she held it by the head and pushed the legs except it's the head that bent and broke.
MN: Ah... I can see how that could happen. What happened for you in your brain when you saw that?
Karen: I was really frustrated and just wanted to scream at her.
MN: So there was some frustration and you wanted to scream at her. What did the frustration make you want to scream?

Karen: It wanted me to scream "GO AWAY" and just be by myself with my broken doll. It was brand new and I liked it sooo much.

MN: It wanted you to scream "Go away" and be by yourself, ...anything else?

Karen: Hum..I think just that, because I was really sad.

MN: So even though that was very tempting, you're telling me that you didn't do that. What did you do instead?

Karen: I just thought that she didn't know her own strength.

MN: So even though anger was really big, you sort of found an excuse for her? (Nods) What allowed you to do that, did you notice something about her?

Karen: Not really.

MN: What did her face look like?

Karen: She looked...hum...she looked...I don't know...I guess she looked really embarrassed.

MN: So you noticed she looked embarrassed? (Nods) Was she saying anything?

Karen: Yeah, now that I think about it she kept on saying "I'm sorry, I'm sorry"...

MN: So you heard her saying sorry. Anything else you could tell about her?

Karen: No, that's it. She just looked embarrassed and kept apologizing.

MN: She looked embarrassed and apologized. Can you guess what else maybe was happening for her inside that was maybe invisible?

Karen: Hum...Well... Maybe... I guess she also looked stunned. I think she was frustrated and disappointed that the doll was broken, maybe she was just like me. She really didn't mean to break it, she just didn't know her own strength.

MN: So your brain saw a lot of things about her: her face looking embarrassed and you guessed that she felt some frustration, surprise and disappointment at not being able to play anymore, just like you. You also realized that her intentions were not to break the doll and you heard her apologies. Is it possible that some of these invisible things that your brain noticed helped you not scream at her?

Karen: Probably, because now that I think about it, I really saw her face and she did seem so sorry ... that really did make a difference for me.

MN: So noticing her face, her "invisibles", and hearing her, helped you not listen to the anger and yell. What would have happened if you had screamed at her?

Karen: I would have ruined my friendship with her and would have been even more sad and then embarrassed too.

MN: You would have had a broken doll and a broken friendship? (Nods) What happened after all of this, were you able to fix it together?

Karen: My friend and I didn't, but my Dad did that night so I was really glad I hadn't yelled at her. She's a really good friend. ....

MN: That's wonderful! So your dad fixed the doll and you saved your friendship!

By considering some visible and invisible aspects of her friend's experience, Karen was able to make a better choice in response to the problem of her broken doll. While she was initially unaware of many of her own observations, the process of discussing these categories will make them more readily accessible to her next time a similar situation arises.

Questions and answers

Question. You stated that these conversations can be fruitful with even young children. Can you really start doing this when they're young?

Answer. First, let me say that this style of conversations is not a technique that I "do" to people. It's really more a set of values by which I like to live; it's an interest in young people's thinking. For this reason, I have had little two-minute exchanges along the lines of SBC with children as young as three or four years old. For example, as I was writing this book, my four-year-old daughter had an incident with one of her park friends. She had climbed a tree with Harry and they were coming down when she noticed a shiny ribbon on the ground and pointed it out to him. Upon seeing it, Harry quickly jumped from the tree and grabbed the ribbon. When my daughter reached the ground, he quickly turned around, clearly intending on keeping it. She kindly said "Harry, I'm the one who saw it, remember? Can you show it to me?" Harry ran away with the ribbon. She stared for a second and then just went back to playing with the other kids in the play structure.

Having witnessed this from a distance, I later asked her if she thought that the ribbon was important for Harry:

Amelia: Yes, I think he maybe had never seen a ribbon!
MN: Was it okay for you that he kept it?
Amelia: Yes, because I've seen many before.
MN: Was that generous that you let him have it?
Amelia (smiles): I guess!
MN: Do you think he was happy?
Amelia: Well, he didn't say anything, but I think he was.

MN: Does it feel good to you to make people happy?
Amelia (smiles): Yes!

She then started to talk about something else. It was my cue that it was enough.

This was a very brief exchange but we covered consideration of herself and other, some implications for this choice, the skill she used and the meaning it could have for the kind of person she liked to be. Notice that I didn't judge or evaluate her choice by saying "good job." This is one of those phrases adults often use with the very best intention of supporting children's successes. But it's important to realize that it often has the opposite effect. Saying "good job" here could have moved her focus away from herself and her relationship with Harry to an experience of having pleased me. Since pleasing a parent is a powerful experience at that age, it would have colonized her burgeoning sense of self. Children raised by a succession of "good job" statements may end up repeating the experience of letting other children keep a finding such as the ribbon in inappropriate situations, later on, just to please an adult, and may lose their own sense of judgment.

CHAPTER 7

The Skill-ionaire in Every Child:
Integrating Social & Emotional Intelligence

"Mommy, I would like to give you this $20 bill grandma gave me for my birthday because I owe you some money for when you bought fishes for my aquarium a month ago. I could have chosen to not say anything, because I know you forgot all about it, but I decided that I actually wanted to be honest."

Mike, 9 years old

Young people who have developed their meta-awareness and big picture understanding are better able to make decisions when faced with an unexpected emotional or social dilemma. They are not bounced around as much by temptations to gain and impulsions to react. They are more likely to be aware of their choices and consider a variety of responses.

In the story above, Mike based his decision on the kind of person he preferred to be. At another time he might have based his decision on not wanting to hurt his parent's feelings or may have considered the importance of trust in the relationship. Mike was able to weight each of these factors differently. What really matters is that he engaged in self-reflection. If you were Mike's parent, you might want to respond by calmly showing appreciation and then perhaps pushing his self-reflection ever so slightly by asking an inconspicuous question.

In fact Mike's mother's response was: "Well, thank you. Do you like the feeling of being honest?" Mike thought about it for a second, nodded, smiled and left to resume his activities.

In a precious moment like this, it is better to ask too little, rather than too many, questions so the young person can fully experience satisfaction rather than annoyance.

From a collection of successes to a skill-ionaire identity

Progressing from the experience of having a series of isolated successes, made visible through SBC, to developing a stable and integrated sense of being compassionate, capable, and generally competent to handle social and emotional dilemmas requires a few extra steps. Mike has been exposed to a number of SBC and is able to make value-based, as opposed to gain-directed, decisions. Before the skills identified through SBC could become integrated into Mike's identity, they had to be:

- experienced as meaningful, not just once but on several occasions
- named to become more distinctively packaged in the brain
- witnessed and acknowledged by a few other people to confirm its existence
- tied to past roots and maybe a future to strengthen their endurance
- connected to an awareness of the context in which they were learned

Let's review in finer detail the process of supporting the development of a confident, competent and response-able young person. Then we'll look at how these skills allow them to develop their social and emotional intelligence.

See it many times

Over time, young people have successes that have some similarities. They often do not notice these similarities, especially if they are young, as they tend to be more present oriented. *Asking them,* if the skill they used in their latest success seemed similar in some ways to the skills they used in another incident, can help build an association in their brains. When a skill is made visible at least three times and stories of successes are interconnected, the brain starts to link the events and young people can start seeing themselves as being skilled in this type of situation. To link successful events, you can ask questions such as:

- You are telling me that you tried to remember that winning wasn't so important and you let go of your disappointment by remembering how much playing is really what matters? Is that similar to what you did a few weeks ago when your team lost a soccer game?
- Does this also have anything to do with the card incident from last month?

Name it

Another way to help young people "wire in" the feeling that they are successful, is to name the skills they used. One-word names are much easier to recall than entire stories. It is easier to think of oneself as "generous" rather than "a person who likes to share her treats, take care of others' needs, and give special presents to her friends." Of course both descriptions are valuable and worth being articulated, but the single word will be easier to evoke in a challenging situation. For example, "I really dislike this student, but I like to be generous so I'll share with her too, just as with everyone else in the class."

With most SBC, it is preferable that young people be the ones to name the skill. If they don't, you can always propose a word, but your suggestion will be fairly useless unless it really fits with their experience and feels meaningful *to them*. To name a skill, you can ask questions such as:

- How would you name the ability to share with someone you don't like very much?
- What would you think of people who are able to share not only with friends but also with others who are lonely, even if they dislike them?
- What would you call people who share easily, even precious items?

The point is to let the naming come from the young person, if at all possible.

Invite others to acknowledge it

If you are the only one who thinks that you are skilled at singing, you might be doubtful about the validity of your perception. If your mother thinks you are skilled at singing, too, then you might give it a bit more credence. Now if the neighbors or a teacher or a wider audience thinks so too, you'd probably be more willing to trust the validity of your skill. The more different people witness a skill, the more it feels valid, reliable and real to us. This is important to SBC as well. To highlight others' observations of success, you can ask questions such as:

- Did anyone notice that you solved this fight without swearing?
- If anyone noticed the progress you made, who might that be?
- I wonder what your teacher would tell me if I called her to share the effort you've been putting into this.
- Do you think we can recount this story to your Dad? I think he would be really pleased!

Give it a past

We often have a past story about our problems (White & Epston, 1990). We can give lots of explanations and historical details about why we are shy, for example. Why not find a past for our skills? Surely they didn't manifest themselves from thin air! Giving them a past makes them significantly more tangible. If you've just discovered that you can be assertive, for example, you will feel a lot more anchored and secure if you recognize the people and experiences who contributed to this. It's the difference between meeting a new date and discovering that your best friend has always loved you. You are far more likely to trust the second scenario and live the experience in a much richer way. Again, the same process helps with young people. To give the success a past, you can ask questions such as:

- Can you think of another time in your life when you were assertive?
- Can you remember a person from your past who could share a story about you being assertive?

- Might there be anyone in your family who wouldn't be surprised to find out that you can be assertive?

Uncover their context

Just as considering the "invisibles" of others during a conflict opens up the possibilities for constructive responses and compassion, uncovering the context that allowed our skills and identity to flourish, balances focus on self and interconnectedness with others. By context, I mean both the people and activities that contributed to the blooming of a person.

Our identity and skills do not develop in a vacuum. They are usually inspired and nurtured by people, and maintained in the context of certain relationships. To uncover the context in which skills have developed, you can ask questions such as:

- Who might have contributed to you learning to be so patient?
- Has there been a time in your life where you just had to be patient because of the circumstances you were living?
- Is there anything that supports you being patient these days?
- What in your life right now keeps you anchored in patience?

Revisiting the skill-ionaire in every child

Every child has a wealth of skills, often buried in their minds and hearts waiting to be noticed. Young people who become aware and confident in their skills become metaphorically like skill-ionaires. They know from experience that they can successfully overcome a variety of obstacles. They are aware that these skills are fluid and constantly evolving in relationships. They have learned to deeply trust that they will have the social and emotional resources, or intelligence, to solve most life challenges.

Having skills doesn't mean that they do not experience uncomfortable and even destructive emotions such as anger. Rather, it means that they are usually able to catch themselves before engaging in harmful actions and instead generate other, more constructive solutions. They can do this because they have learned to simultaneously consider themselves and others, keep problems small, and quickly evaluate the consequences of each option. This social agility is illustrated in the story below about one of my teenage clients who enjoys playing soccer.

"I was just scoring an amazing goal, which meant our team was winning, when the referee blew his whistle and called it an off side and a "no-goal." I felt really, really angry because it wasn't an off side in my opinion. The anger was so intense that, weirdly, it occurred to me that I was stronger and bigger than him. Without even thinking about what I'd do exactly, I started racing angrily towards him. He was looking the other way so he couldn't see me approaching until the last minute when he turned around. He was quite startled to see me a few feet away from him. I saw his face. He was scared. In the meantime I was also hearing myself think more and more clearly, "What am I doing?? This is a bad idea!" Coming back to my senses, I became very clear that it would be sooo unlike me to do anything harmful. ... but it was too late to stop, it was impossible because I had way too much speed ... so I hugged him!! He was quite stunned and an uproar of laughter erupted from the audience! I quickly went back to my position before he could ask me any questions!"

While this young man was obviously overtaken at first by his frustration, he was nevertheless able to skillfully transform the problem his anger had triggered into a creative action that better represented his own clear preference for non-violence, his respect for the referee and his dream of becoming a professional soccer player.

All children can develop their emotional intelligence

The concept of emotional intelligence was first described by Salovey & Meyer (1990), who defined it as accurately and adaptively perceiving, understanding or expressing emotions of the self or others. In 1995 the writer Daniel Goleman popularized and expanded the concept in his aptly named book *Emotional Intelligence.*

As discussed in our previous chapter, young people can develop what is known as meta-awareness, which allows them to recognize and label their internal emotional experience of an event. Such labeling can be difficult because many physiological markers are not necessarily linked to a specific emotion (Kagan, 2007). In other words, when your heart rate or respiration increases, it can be for very different reasons; you could equally be excited, anxious or fearful. Children not only have to read their own body cues accurately but also sort out what these physiological markers actually *mean to them.* This contributes to the fact that different children often react totally differently to the same situation.

This is further complicated by the fact that experience of emotions are linked to the biological development of different sections of the brain, which are believed to mature at different times. The primitive limbic system develops rapidly early in life and is responsible for the expression of basic emotions (distress, excitement, rage, joy) while the frontal regions of the cerebral cortex develop later and are associated with the ability to exert control (Lewis & Steiben, 2004).

The expression of many basic emotions is thought to be universal. People's facial expression of joy, for example, will look the same no matter where you go (Ekman, 2007). We see this most dramatically in children who are blind at birth and have never observed a smile or a frown, who nevertheless smile and frown in the same way that sight-privileged people do (Goldsmith, 2002). While the basic expressions are the same, the social rules around expressing these emotions appropriately (i.e. the when, where, why, to whom, how) often vary greatly from one culture to another (Shiraev & Levy, 2007). For example, in North America and Europe we consider it acceptable to have long and intense expressions of emotions, while in several East Asian countries emotions tend to be concealed in the presence of others, especially unpleasant emotions, which might disrupt group cohesiveness (Shiraev & Levy, 2007). It takes many of the very skills emphasized in SBC to be able to determine socially appropriate contexts for expressing certain emotions.

Because of the neuroplasticity of the brain, children who grow up in a supportive environment that encourages self-reflection, awareness and emotional skills, develop at a younger age, greater abilities to monitor and control the biological intensity of their emotions (Siegel & Hartzell, 2004). Studies have shown that, parents who view uncomfortable emotions as opportunities to label experience, ask questions, support, and discuss strategies, tend to have children who are more skilled at physiologically soothing themselves, better able to focus their attention and have fewer behavioral problems (Gottman, 2008). In other words, these children develop the ability to take into consideration the emotional experiences of self and others, also called attunement, and respond to interactions in flexible ways (Siegel, 1999).

Self-Monitoring, Self-Regulation

"I was so disappointed when I read the cast list and realized that I didn't get to have the role of Aladdin. It was tempting to walk away and be rude to the person who got it. Then I realized that he didn't even know I wanted it and he actually had nothing to do with me not getting the role. So I decided to be "normal" with him and just told myself that I'd try out again for a big role next year. Maybe I can enjoy the role I did get."

Jerry, 13 years old

Once young people become experienced in meta- awareness, of theirs and others' emotions, they will begin to be able to recognize and label experiences within a matter of seconds, leaving much mental power for the next step: self-monitoring. Self-monitoring, also called self-regulation, is an important part of emotional intelligence as it requires that young people be capable of managing their biological arousal in any given situation (Thompson, Meyer & Jochem, 2008). Self-monitoring of emotions can be measured by four variables (Ekman, 2007):

1. Intensity: the strength or force of the biological activation associated with the emotion (quality)
2. Frequency: the number of times an individual experiences an emotion in a given time frame (quantity)

3. Length: the duration of the peak emotional experience
4. Recovery: the time needed to return to the usual emotional baseline

Young people aware of their socio-emotional skills have integrated abilities that allow them to:

1. Contemplate many explanations for a problem situation and therefore be less deeply captured by an upsetting interpretation (less intense)
2. Be more grounded in calm and therefore less reactive to the ups and downs of life (less frequent emotional upsets)
3. Have a repertoire of tools to reduce the duration of unpleasant emotions at their peak (shorter length)
4. Return more quickly to their emotional baseline since the intensity was low in the first place and they are optimistic about being able to resolve problems (quicker recovery)

This is illustrated in the example described above of the middle school boy who had been anxiously waiting to find out the results of his audition for the school play.

In this example, Jerry took care of his own feelings of frustration by limiting its:

1. Intensity (de-escalating his biological activation about the experience)
2. Frequency (internally reducing the frustrating self-talk automatically reduces the frequency of its outburst with regards to this issue)

3. Duration (problem solving ideas and consideration of others' "invisibles" were generated quickly, leading to an immediate reduction of the frustration)
4. Recovery period (reconnecting with his preferred way of being positive and enthusiastic about being in the play)

It can be said that young people who have experienced SBC develop a strong emotional anchor. They know how they prefer to be and only move very slightly when blown by emotional winds. They can remain somewhat grounded and maintain an optimistic view of people and the world. This optimistic view, and trust that there is a solution to all problems, leaves young people less vulnerable to intense destructive emotions. It allows them to proceed more slowly through problems and seek solutions, since there always are solutions, to all problems.

Every child can develop social intelligence

The concept of social intelligence was first proposed in the 1920s by psychologist Edward Thorndike, who defined it as an ability to understand and manage people of all ages. As with the concept of emotional intelligence, this idea was later popularized by Howard Gardner (1993) and Daniel Goleman (2006). These authors redefined social intelligence as involving two main aspects:

1. social awareness, which includes empathy and the ability to infer what others are thinking and feeling
2. social facility, which includes self-presentation and the ability to have a positive influence on the resolution of tensions.

142

Various models have been proposed to analyze the actual process of handling social events (Dodge, 1993). In SBC, young people's brains are primed for the many complex parts of interactions, including:

1. noticing cues that matter

2. accurately interpreting and making sense of the information

3. generating options for response

4. predicting the likely outcome of these various responses

5. selecting a response which fits with the person they prefer to be

6. appropriately engaging in the selected response

7. adjusting the response based on the reaction of the other person

Young people who are invited into SBC develop their social awareness and better understand others' "invisibles." They have an enhanced ability to resolve social tensions because they have noticed their own wide range of successful strategies while reviewing their successes. They tend to see good intentions and "invisibles" in others, which allows them to have a positive view of others and assume that everyone is simply doing the best they can given the circumstances of their lives. Such a perspective opens the space for a sense of shared responsibility in resolving problems instead of blaming others.

This process is illustrated in the following story of 10-year-old Annie, who is handling an upsetting situation with her sister with great social intelligence.

"I did all the work to set up the table for dinner, which normally gives me the right to sit in our special comfy swivel chair. But when I came back into the dining room, after my last trip in the kitchen, I found my sister sitting in it. I almost yelled at her in frustration, but then I stopped, 'cause I realized that if I did we would have a fight and then all four of us would get into it and then it would ruin one of our rare dinners all together. I also saw that she seemed to be in a big hurry and I remembered that she was leaving soon to see a movie with her friends. I decided to just let it go, which was good because I actually got to hear a funny story about her friends."

Specifically, Annie displayed social intelligence by:

1. noticing cues that matter: her sister was in a hurry
2. accurately interpreting and making sense of the information: her sister needed to leave soon and was eating quickly
3. generating options for response: she could yell or let it go
4. predicting the likely outcome of these various responses: yelling would lead to a fight and loss of precious family dinner time; letting it go could lead to precious and enjoyable family time
5. selecting a response that fit with the person she preferred to be: let it go because values family time
6. appropriately engaging in the selected response: just sat elsewhere

7. adjust her response based on the reaction of the other person and embrace the funny stories told by her sister instead of pouting.

A number of studies have shown that girls display more pro-social behaviors than boys (Einsenberg, Fabes & Spinrad, 2006). It is difficult to disentangle these results from the socialization of girls to be caregivers. In my experience, boys can certainly be encouraged to develop their experiences of empathy and pro-social responses.

As would be expected, young people who have developed social intelligence are more likely to make good friends and are rarely disliked by their peers. They are often considered "popular," which, research shows, often implies being supportive of others, expressing appreciation, listening attentively, communicating readily, controlling their emotions, acting like themselves, and being enthusiastic and self-confident (Rubin, Bukowski & Parker, 2006; Saarni & colleagues, 2006).

Questions and Answers

Question. You have explained many ways of supporting children's socio-emotional skills. Are there things we should avoid doing?

Answer. Yes, tweaking people's experience of themselves is serious business. It is important to be very clear about your intentions. Do you really want to do this because it is best for the child? SBC used for purposes other than the well-being of youth do not work very well.

In addition to your intentions, you must also thoughtfully examine the potential effect of the words you are planning to use. The following statement is an example of commonly used and well-intended message that can have real negative effects and move children away from developing their own internal wealth: *"You're the best, you're so much faster than anyone else on your team."* This statement, while meant to be supportive, praises only by comparison. It measures accomplishment by putting down others. Words like these will tend to keep a young person feeling only a tenuous sense of worth. Once this young person meets a "faster" child – and this will inevitably happen –his or her sense of pride and accomplishment will go out the window. Such statements are also isolating. They set up young people against their friends and teammates, who in some ways become threats or "enemies" to their self-worth.

It is much safer to support young people in feeling satisfied with their own performance and proud of having done the best they could. This encourages them to evaluate their performance in relation to their own values, beliefs and preferences, not that of others. Young people who have experienced SBC are able to articulate what is important to *them* and the kind of person *they* prefer to be. They can tell you all about why they prefer to be a certain way and why they like it. And that, ultimately, is our goal.

Question. Would telling a child that she has a math "gene" help her notice her abilities and boost her confidence in facing increasingly complex math problems?

Answer. I really appreciate the intention behind this question – the desire to help children trust their own abilities.

Unfortunately, the genetic explanation, because it involves a fixed, static notion of a talent, can be risky. It can leave the youth feeling vulnerable, as it conceals the things she herself did to contribute to her success, such as practice.

Extensive research by scientists including Stanford University professor Carol Dweck (2005) has shown that an *overemphasis* on a fixed internal identity leaves young people fearful of challenges and mistakes that can become threats to their sense of self-worth. When they do face the unavoidable failures of life, they attribute them to a lack of internal skills, give up and remain passive, instead of trying harder. They feel powerless in their abilities to effect change and often become defensive when receiving feedback. In other words, they end up believing that if something is hard to master, it means that they are not very intelligent, when in fact challenges are just part of learning.

It is much safer to support the specific skills and action that were taken to accomplish the success, such as: "You really worked hard on that assignment and it paid off!" "Scoring that goal took such determination. You kept on running and running." "You were so persistent in explaining yourself clearly to your father yesterday."

Young people who are aware of their skills feel confident about their ability to try things and work through hardships, and when they don't succeed, it is not overwhelming because failures do not drain their sense of worthiness as a person. They know they are able to learn, and have recognized on a number of occasions the complex mix between helpful thoughts and non-helpful thoughts. They are able to see this simply as a part of life and not as suggesting something negative about who they are.

What matters most, then, is the process not the outcome. What is important is the act of learning or bettering oneself as a person, not the measure of performance such as a grade or a score. I am reminded of the exciting science fairs that go on each year in many school districts. Young people work very hard, for many weeks, at researching, creating, and sharing a special experiment that fascinates them personally. For many youth, this community sharing is all very exhilarating and growth promoting until a principal decides to give worthless ribbons for first, second and third place projects. Then you see smiles disappear and disappointment grow. Suddenly the excitement of working hard, making mistakes, learning and sharing the joy of discovery is usurped by competition. In general, the effort matters more than the accomplishment.

Question. Can you really help a kindergartner develop empathy with SBC?

Answer. Yes, and the development of empathy, the ability to put oneself in another's shoes and feel an emotional response that is similar to the other's feelings (DamonS, 1988; Santrock, 2009), is of particular importance in SBC. In our last story, Annie displayed empathy by recognizing that her sister was in a hurry and allowing her to sit in the swivel chair without comment.

Of course Annie was 10 years old, not a kindergartner. At 10, her capacity for empathy is becoming richer because of the more complex connections being formed in the brain. But kindergartners can also be encouraged to develop empathy. For example, at the time of writing of this book, my four years old was getting a little exasperated with my forgetfulness and reduced attunement to her needs. As I was getting breakfast organized for everyone one weekday morning, she stomped her foot impatiently on the ground, frowned her little face and said: "Mommy, I've asked you nicely for a glass of milk many times now and you still haven't given it to me. I'm thirsty!" I smiled, acknowledged she was right, apologized, headed towards the milk and then playfully asked her: "Can you guess why I didn't give it to you yet?"

Amelia (thinking): "Because you were busy making my snack for pre-school?"
MN: "Yes, and what else?"
Amelia: "Because maybe you didn't hear me all three times because you were talking with Daddy?"
MN (finally giving her the milk): "Yes and what else?"
Amelia: "Because you're preparing my brother for school and thinking of your book?"
MN: "That's exactly right! I'm doing all these things at once in my head even though it's not visible when you look at me. I'm sorry it got in the way of me listening to you. Thanks for understanding."

My little one smiled. Her developing brain further recorded the fact that people have "invisibles" which can get in the way of smooth interactions. This is another seed of empathy planted in her brain.

In sum, most school-age children can be encouraged to develop empathy, but they will experience their own unique version of it depending on the development of their brain and the environment they are exposed to. In toddlers, it may be visible by their expression of genuine concern for others even if they are unable to take effective action. In early childhood, empathy is displayed by an understanding of multiple perspectives and an ability to respond somewhat soothingly to people's distress; by adolescence, empathy can be experienced on a more global level, extend to people we don't know and be evoked for humanitarian issues such as poverty (Berger, 2009).

CHAPTER 8

Using SBC for Socio-Emotional Problems: What Should be Done Differently?

Sheilagh, 7, speaks only to her family members and has been diagnosed with selective mutism. Her parents and teachers have talked to her, encouraged her to speak and implemented various rewards and consequence-based programs to encourage her speaking. All to no avail.

Thomas, 12, tends to be jealous of his 7-year-old brother and constantly showers him with comments such as, "you're so stupid," "you're ugly," "you wouldn't even know basic math such as how to multiply 11 by 11."

Kelly, 14, has been subjected to alcohol-related violence throughout the first six years of her life. She struggles with anxiety disorders such as obsessions, phobias and flashbacks. She reports feeling "messed up" and struggles with a lot of hatred, particularly towards her father.

SBC can be helpful with most young people given the right time and place. If there is an actual problem, and especially if it directly affects your relationship with the young person, other types of conversations may be beneficial before engaging in SBC. This is particularly true if the problem has been longstanding and involves anger, disconnection or distrust.

The longer the problem has been around, the more complex the neural pathways in the brain. The brain fires to the biggest, thickest, and fastest neural pathway that can be applied to a situation, especially if it is triggered in an unexpected situation. So if your child typically responds in a mean way to his or her sibling, it will take some time to weaken the habit, and strengthen the neural network associated with a more patient response. This biological mechanism can make the process of changing established behavioral patterns more complex and may require the assistance of a savvy psychologist or counselor.

The work in this book is derived from narrative therapy, which also offers a number of helpful ways to approach problems. While it is beyond the scope of this book to present these practices in detail, I would like to provide a glimpse of some basic practices. Readers interested in gaining a more in-depth understanding of these practices are encouraged to read my previous book (Beaudoin & Taylor, 2009), which provides an easy-to-read overview of conversations targeting problems. A number of other, wonderful books presenting in more depth the theory behind narrative therapy are also available, such as those published by Michael White (2007), Zimmerman & Dickerson (1996), Freedman & Combs (1996), Nylund (2000), and Freeman, Epston & Lobovits (1997), to name only a few.

Whenever you endeavor to engage children in a conversation in order to help them with a problem, it is important to take caution to ensure that the conversation is indeed reinforcing skills and not strengthening the problem. In this chapter, we will first look at how problems operate in the brain, and then I will nuance the applications of SBC in these particular contexts.

How problems operate

Problems tend to be associated with unpleasant emotions, and these emotions are among the fastest and most powerful memories to be encoded in the brain. Once these memories are triggered by an interaction or a certain context, trying to halt them is like trying to stop a freight train at its maximum speed.

Why don't problems just go away when we want them to?

Problems seem to stick around, no matter how much we might want a trouble-free life. This occurs even when people seek therapeutic help, have fruitful discussions and are very motivated to change. The explanation for why it can take time to change our emotional responses has four brain-related components:

1. The neural pathway for the problem is dense and fast.
2. The neural pathway for the problem is connected to a sense of identity through time.
3. The neural pathway for the new behavior is weak and thin.
4. The neural pathway for the new behavior is either not meaningful enough or lacks connections with other meaningful memories.

1. The neural pathway for the problem is dense and fast.

As illustrated in figure 8.1, a problem neural pathway can be like a highway that carries information very quickly in your brain. For example, have you ever tried changing the password on your email account? If you have, you know what I mean by an established, fast, neural pathway. It literally took me a few weeks to correctly enter my new password right upon opening my account. Whenever I would try to make a quick check of my email, especially if I was in a hurry, it was guaranteed I'd enter the old, invalid password. This is for a small, mundane detail of life that has no emotions attached, doesn't threaten any established relationship, and says nothing about my identity.

If changing a small habitual behavior like typing an email password is hard, imagine how hard it is to change more established, problem neural pathways – and how much more time and patience it takes. All people, young and old, encounter this difficulty when trying to change an established response, such as those described in the stories of Sheilagh, Thomas and Kelly.

Figure 8.1. The neural pathway for the problem is dense and fast

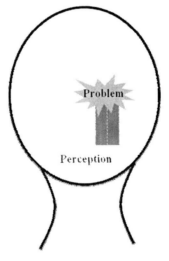

2. The neural pathway for the problem is connected to an identity.

Now let's imagine that I had some emotional baggage attached to my example above. If I had a poor opinion of myself as having a bad memory or being unskilled with computers, the password change issue would hook onto this complex and powerful network in my brain and associated with an uncomfortable emotion of inadequacy. The incident would no longer be just an annoying password change but rather would represent something more serious and problematic about the kind of person I am. As illustrated in figure 8.2, the problem would become connected in the brain with a bigger problem story of myself, a problem identity, which would make it much harder to change. This is was the case for Sheilagh.

While most people have experiences of self-consciousness here and there and make nothing of it, Sheilagh had been labeled with a diagnosis that connected the problem to her identity. Everyone's reaction to her silence loaded the neural pathways associated with social interaction with discomfort and a sense of being inadequate, thus making it increasingly difficult for her to deviate from the problem neural pathway and speak spontaneously.

Figure 8.2. The neural pathway for the problem is connected to an identity

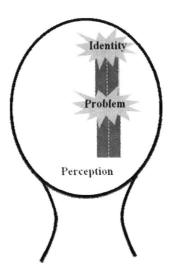

3. The neural pathway for the preferred response is weak and thin.

The neural pathway for the preferred behavior has typically been used less often, noticed less by others and may have less intense emotions attached to it. As illustrated in figure 8.3, the likelihood that the brain would choose this particular pathway is very slim, especially in unexpected situations that require a quick response. Thomas' experience provides an example of this scenario. The neural pathway for generosity and care exists in Thomas, but especially in relationship to his sibling, it has been triggered less often in his brain and remains weak and thin. In other words, it's far less likely that the brain would choose this pathway over the more deeply embedded, thicker, stronger and more problematic reactions, which have been triggered so often.

Figure 8.3. The neural pathway for the preferred response is weak and thin

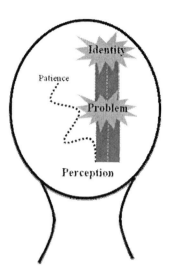

4. The neural pathway for the preferred response is either not meaningful enough or lacks connections with other meaningful memories.

In some cases the neural pathway for the preferred response already exists and is used occasionally, but has not been noticed or considered meaningful enough to become significant. As illustrated in figure 8.4, the young person may experience the wish to be a certain way (preferred identity) and behaves occasionally in this preferred way without realizing it. There is no connection in the brain between a preferred action taken and its implications with regards to the preferred identity. This is the case for Kelly, for example, who understandably remains captured by all the memories of trauma she has endured and what they mean about her identity. She has not attributed much significance to other experiences in her life, in part because no one noticed them.

Figure 8.4. The neural pathway for the preferred response is either not meaningful enough or lacks connection with a preferred identity and related memories.

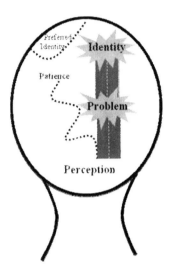

Making Change happen in the brain

Like adults, young people can feel very stuck in their problems and be accused unfairly of not trying, when in reality they would much prefer to stay away from problems. Even though they may rationally know exactly what they're "supposed to do" or even what they'd prefer to do, they often feel unable to stop the freight train of reactions when it is triggered unexpectedly in their minds. In order to effectively help a young person change the programs operating in their brains, caring adults can:

1. Highlight the young person's successes often enough to significantly strengthen that preferred neural pathway and enrich it with awareness and pleasant emotions.

2. Help the young person notice whether or not he likes the more constructive response and articulate why it may be meaningful to him or why it fits with the kind of person he wants to be, thus connecting the preferred neural pathway to a sense of identity.

3. Reduce their own emotional reactivity to the problem when it does occur, if at all possible, thus progressively reducing the strength of the problem neural pathway. Adults can also avoid contexts and situations that are likely to trigger the problem neural pathway.

4. Help young people articulate why they do not like the problem and what they value instead.

The application of the four ideas is illustrated in figure 8.5: The neural pathway for the preferred response is thicker, faster, and connected to a preferred identity with its many related memories. The problem neural pathway is weakened and disconnected from a sense of identity. Over time the problem neural pathway may simply fade away while the preferred neural pathway will become more established (figure 8.6).

Figure 8.5 The neural pathway for the preferred response is thicker and connected to a preferred identity. The problem neural pathway is weakened and disconnected from identity.

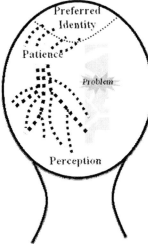

Figure 8.6. Over time the problem neural pathway may simply fade away while the preferred neural pathway will become more established.

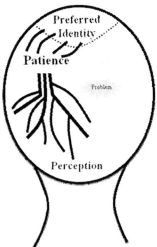

We will now examine how these brain-related facts apply to SBC and the guiding principles discussed in chapter 1.

Reviewing the three guiding principles of SBC

1. A problem doesn't mean a lack of skills: It may mean something is in the way of using one's skills.

Helping a young person move away from a problem may require an understanding of what nourishes the problem, i.e., what contributes to keeping the problem neural pathway so dense and fast. Simply engaging in SBC will not be effective if certain interactions or situations continue to feed the problem.

A good example of this can be seen in the case of Sheilagh, who is struggling with selective mutism. Selective mutism usually has to do with an inability to speak to people outside the family which only worsens with pressure to do so. Children with this problem feel unable to respond verbally and can be very self-conscious. Parents, feeling ashamed or uncomfortable with their child's silence, often inadvertently put pressure on their children to respond socially in hopes of solving the problem.

Since many children, like Sheilagh, are already struggling with their own discomfort, the additional pressure of their parents' or other adults' emotional reactions leaves them progressively more paralyzed mentally in social situations. If not done carefully, a SBC at this point, with its emphasis on "successes," might only worsen the situation.

When such a chronic problem is present, I suggest drawing a picture of the pattern of interaction to better understand the problem. As you can see in figure 8.7, a pattern of interaction involves examining the reciprocal effects of people's behaviors on one another. For example, the more parents focus on their child's inability to speak, the more self-conscious the child becomes and the less able to speak. The less the child speaks, the more parents feel embarrassed socially or worried and, sometimes without realizing it, overly encourage or pressure the child to speak. This creates a pattern of interaction or a vicious cycle that repeats itself over and over again.

Figure 8.7. Patterns of interaction highlight interactions which may inadvertently feed a problem

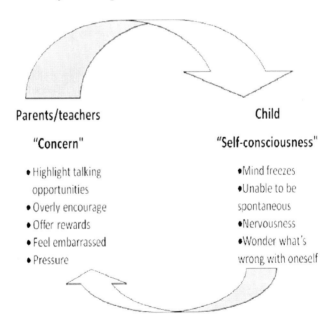

Parents/teachers	Child
"Concern"	"Self-consciousness"
• Highlight talking opportunities	•Mind freezes
• Overly encourage	•Unable to be spontaneous
• Offer rewards	•Nervousness
• Feel embarrassed	•Wonder what's
• Pressure	wrong with oneself

If you understand the self-consciousness involved in selective mutism, then engaging in SBC about successes may not help at all. It may simply exacerbate the self-consciousness. The solution here lies more in the withdrawal of the pressure rather than in the reinforcement of the abilities.

There are many such vicious cycles in which families get stuck. Another common example is when a teenager rebels and reacts angrily to family members, even going as far as running away. If the young person's problem is understood as anger, then the effect of parents' reaction to punish is to inadvertently exacerbate the anger. Parents feel stuck and engage in the only response they can think of, which often replicates what they learned themselves as children and may be ineffective given the problem. In such a situation, the pattern of interaction has to be halted before SBC can be effective.

Parents may not feel very powerful, but they are nevertheless the holders of much of the physical, emotional and financial power within the family. When parents change their own response in the pattern of interaction in a noticeable way, it is likely that young people will end up modifying their responses as well. Moreover, in situations where young people are very angry at and disconnected from their parents, noticing and commenting on their successes without addressing the contributors to the anger, might irritate them more. Adults wanting to check whether or not SBC would be helpful can ask themselves the following questions:

- What responses am I likely to get if I start noting the child's successes? Is the young person likely to be pleased, annoyed or feel scrutinized?
- Does my relationship with this young person allow me to point out and constructively discuss what I notice in his socio-emotional responses?

- If there is a problem, what is this problem about and what patterns of interaction may influence its course?

2. Important efforts and skills are hidden by problems: Externalizing can help

As illustrated a number of times in this book, a really helpful aspect of self-awareness is the recognition of the complexity and at times contradictory nature of our thoughts. In more simple terms, recognizing that we can experience different "parts" of ourselves thinking different things can open the door to many possibilities of response. Such awareness is really helpful as it provides a canvas for understanding the complexity and multifaceted nature of experience.

For example, when you are angry, the anger part of you may make you feel tempted to scream an insult while another part of you is clear that you should not do that. Awareness of these different experiences allows you to gain more control over various situations. It enables you to reduce the strength of the connection between the problem neural pathway and your identity. If anger is only one of many experiences you have of yourself, then it cannot accurately represent your identity.

For example, Thomas tends to respond to social situations with patience and empathy but utters rather mean statements when facing the same type of annoyances with his sibling. In such a situation, in addition to the patterns of interaction discussed above, Thomas can be invited to reflect on the kind of person he becomes when listening to "Impatience." Externalizing language in this way is particularly useful in helping the young person gain perspective on his or her response.

What externalizing involves is simply talking about the problem as something external to the person's identity (White & Epston, 1990). The problem becomes like a virus or a habit, so to speak, that can be examined as something separate from who the person is. It does not represent the person. Externalizing language allows you to acknowledge clearly that you know the child is not behaving at her or his best and is simply stuck in a reaction, habit or unpleasant emotion. It also provides a linguistic method to recognize that a child's program for responding to life originated outside of his or her intentions i.e. most of children's reactions have been learned through interactions with their caregivers and the various people in their environment. Consequently, these learned problem responses cannot be taken as a representation of who they'd prefer to be.

In practice, externalizing language creates a context where young people can be more "response-able." If the problem does not represent who they are, they then have the choice to take control of the problem response and change it in order to be more congruent with who they prefer to be.

In an externalizing conversation, for example, Thomas can be asked if he experiences some *"Frustration"* at his brother. Once the problem is named, other questions can be asked such as: "Does the *Frustration* make you want to push him"? "Does the *Frustration* make you forget that he's younger and doesn't know certain things yet?" Does the *Frustration* make you forget the fun you had with him this morning?" Does the *Frustration* make you do things you might later regret?" etc.

Hearing this enough times leaves young people better able to reflect on their unpleasant emotion and better able to consider responding differently using their existing socio-emotional skills. When the problem is actually named, SBC can then be used to show how they controlled the *Frustration*.

The practice of externalizing was also illustrated in chapter 5 with the SBC example of my son waking up from a nightmare. In that situation, I had externalized *"Fear."* This externalization contributed to him gaining perspective on what was happening and letting go of the imaginary dangers.

3. Broadening the scope from a problem to a person focus: The bigger the problem, the more skills to uncover

Young people may appear to be captured by a problem behavior 100% of the time or to be drowning under the weight of intense emotions associated with depression, fears or traumas. Since no one tolerates suffering passively, there are always times when they are successful at managing the problem or at the very least times when the problem is less present.

Young people struggling with problems may not have fully articulated the implications of their behaviors with regards to the kind of person they are becoming or could become. Their preference for problem solving and awareness of their skills may be buried under the clutter of uncomfortable emotions. In such situations, it can be extremely important to pay attention to their successes and collect several meaningful examples of skills they used to overcome problems. Articulating such examples can enrich preferred neural pathways. It allows these pathways to become both denser and connected to a number of stories about their preferred identities.

I would like to end this book with the transcript of the third conversation I had with Kelly who, you'll recall, endured great trauma. I'm including this story to illustrate the presence of skills even in situations that may at first appear hopeless. No child's situation is entirely hopeless. It is important to take great care when working with children and adolescents who have endured trauma. Jumping too quickly into conversations focused solely on skills can easily be experienced as disrespectful.

Today Kelly shares her experience of feeling "messed up for life" because of her parents' violence in her first 6 years, before she was placed in foster care. As a child she was given a diagnostic of Obsessive Compulsive Disorder and later, placed in a Special Education Program. In the last few years her father has regained custody of her and her sister, even though he still struggles with occasional alcoholism. He has made great efforts and progress through therapeutic conversations, but Kelly still profoundly hates and distrusts him. Today she comes in and talks about her frequent flashbacks to the beatings she endured as a child.

> *K: I always have flashbacks of the beatings.*
> *MN: Do you have them every day?*
> *K: Yes.*
> *MN: How do you stop them?*
> *K:They just fade in and out. I don't have control of them.*
> *They are very vivid; I see everything very clearly: my*
> *mother's make-up running as she's crying and beating me,*
> *my father drunk and scary...*
> *MN: Are there any flashbacks that you can sometimes stop?*
> *K: There's one that I can from when I was 6.*
> *MN: How do you stop it?*

K: I don't know. I just let it go.
MN: How do you let it go?
K: It's like if I was pulling a long rope of memories through time and so I try to pass the bad scene.
MN: So you pull the rope of memories, pass the bad scene and get to some other scenes?
K: Yes.
MN: Like what other scenes, for example?
K: Oh, just my cat...I had a cat named Bagera.
MN: Bagera? (Nods) Like in the jungle story? (She smiles and nods)
MN: I used to have a cat, too. What did your cat look like?
K: It was black and orange and she was actually the mother of others. We had 10 cats. We also had a dog named Moski and two birds. My sister's was green and mine was blue, and her name was Sheeba.
MN: Did Sheeba and Bagera support you in the moments of hardships? How might they have supported you?
K: Well, Sheeba was mostly pretty to look at. But Bagera supported me. I held her when I was scared and she slept with me.
MN: In my experience, cats are really picky about who they like. What did Bagera see in you that made her so close to you?
K: She saw that I was small like a cat and (hesitatingly) ...that I tried to imitate her positions laying down.
MN(amused): You tried to lie down like her?
K: (smiles and nods): Sometimes I also put a leash on her and ran to the neighbor's house so we could see some of her kitties.
MN: Was she motherly to her kittens?
K: Yes, at first she was.
MN: Was she also motherly to you in some cat way? (nods)

K: She licked my hair and she woke me up in the morning 4-5 minutes before someone would wake me up. She would purr really loudly in my ear.

MN: Was that helpful to you that she did that?

K: Yes. it gave me more time to get ready for school.

MN: What is it that you did that made her take care of you in those ways?

K: I would spend time with her, I didn't chase her, I let her come to me and I was never mean to her.

MN: You were never mean to her even though people were mean to you?

K: No! She never hurted me. Why would I hurt her? The humans were the ones mean to me, not the animals.

MN: Often kids who are beaten and subjected to violence end up in turn being mean to small animals; they sort of take it out on creatures weaker than they are.

K: I could never do that, I knew it would be wrong. I did the opposite. I even saved a squirrel one day when his leg was stuck in the fence.

MN: You saved a squirrel? (nods) How did you avoid being bitten? Trapped animals are often very aggressive with humans when they're trapped.

K: He didn't bite me. I have a special connection with animals. I understand their language.

MN: Would you say they trust you?

K: Yes, they trust me.

MN: What do you think about the fact that you endured a lot of violence and instead of turning around and hurting small animals like many do, you were actually kind and caring to them?

K (puzzled and hesitant): ....I guess that...(unsure) that... would be a good trait...wouldn't it?

MN: I would see it as a good trait. What would this "good trait" mean about you?

K (very puzzled): I guess... it would mean that...I fought stronger things... and cared for weaker things?!?!

MN: If a small child is able to fight stronger things and care for weaker things, what does that say about the child? What does it take for the child to do that?

K (slowly then excited): ...I imagine some kind of strength...You know I also learned to read on my own because I was really fascinated by animals. My dad never believed it because I was too scared to read out loud. My favorite animals were wolves, whales and saber tooth tigers. I really enjoyed drawing them too...

Kelly becomes excited to discover what she sees as "strengths" in herself and starts recalling other memories that would fit in this category. She sees herself as skilled perhaps for the first time in her life. Seeing herself as skilled opens the door to new ways of thinking and hopes for a brighter future.

Kelly started the conversation feeling "messed up for life' and ended it feeling skilled and strong. No matter how difficult the situation, no matter how many challenges were faced, *you* can help a child find his or her own inner wealth of skills, because there is

A Skill-ionaire in Every Child....

Conclusion

I hope that the ideas shared in this book have left you both interested in having conversations with young people and intrigued by their skills.

As you begin to digest these ideas and put them into practice, you may find yourself noticing your own successes as well as those of your family members. When you cultivate appreciation, it does have a tendency to grow and spread!

I am delighted and honored to contribute this small seed of appreciation in the world. We tend to forget that happiness doesn't come as a result of getting something we don't have, but rather of recognizing, appreciating and highlighting what is already there (Frederic Koenig).

While our journey together is coming to an end, you may still be wondering how Rita, whose story was shared in the introduction, actually managed to keep her coolness and love of her pink shoes in spite of her friend Genny's insult. Well, from the SBC that followed, we discovered that Rita had a small moment of feeling the sting of Self-Doubt and the temptation to "freak out," run away from the school, and return her shoes. Instead, she immediately tried to think of Genny's "invisibles" and generate big picture explanations. Rita remembered that Genny was jealous of her new boyfriend and privileged status in the group. She also considered the possibility that Genny may have had a "bad week-end." Rita decided to maintain her own opinion. As she said, "I came up with excuses for Genny, and it helped me take care of myself." Rita made herself a beautiful day and refused the invitation to jump into the drama puddle of middle school.

As the Dalai Lama once said: "With realization of one's own potential and self confidence in one's ability, one can build a better humanity."

I wish all of you many "success-full" conversations with the children in your lives.

Summary

SBC is a remarkably powerful and effective way to help children grow. It is not, however, the answer to every issue of childhood and may feel at times uncomfortable to initiate. Just noticing successes is already a big step. What you do next will depend on your relationship to the child, the time, place, the child's comfort level, etc. Just remember that once you notice a success, you have many options. You can:

- do nothing other than enjoy witnessing a child's skills in action
- express appreciation
- acknowledge that the person's action had positive effects and then perhaps recount the story of the successful event to others, in front of the child (making sure this is experienced positively and not as an embarrassment)
- engage in a SBC right there and then
- engage in SBC later when the time and context seem more conducive.

At first you will probably have to stop each time and consider what to do. Over time, as you practice SBC, you will get a feel for what to do when, and eventually it will come more naturally.

When you do choose to initiate SBC with young people, it is important to remember that their growth will happen at its own pace and in unpredictable increments. They may, for example:

1. Notice that they can sometimes handle situations successfully, even though they're not sure how.

2. Replicate some of the strategies discussed in SBC, but also sometimes forget, since their neural pathways for the strategies are not fully established yet.
3. Use some of the SBC-discussed ideas inconsistently but in a growing number of situations.
4. Grasp a big-picture understanding of the situation and the kind of person they prefer to be
5. Develop a sense that they can handle situations well most of the time and feel more calm, confident and skilled in facing the socio-emotional dilemmas of everyday life.

Remember, don't expect 100% immediate success or movement in a straight line. SBC is a journey. If you just practice noticing successes, you will eventually notice the enriching impact of SBC.

References

Anderman. E. & Wolters, C. (2006). Goals, values, and affect: Influence on student motivation. In P. Alexander & P. Winne (Eds.), *Handbook of educational psychology*. Maywah, NJ: Lawrence Erlbaum Assoc. Publ.

Beaudoin, M.N. (2005). Agency and choice in the face of trauma: A narrative therapy map. *Journal of Systemic Therapies*, 24(4), 32-50.

Beaudoin, M.N. & Taylor, M. (2009). *Responding to the culture of bullying and disrespect: New perspectives on collaboration, compassion & responsibility*. Thousand Oaks, CA: Corwin Press.

Begley, S. (2007). *Train your mind, Change your brain*. New York: Ballantine Books.

Berger, K.S. (2009). *The developing person through childhood and adolescence*. New York: Worth Publisher.

Bjork, R. (1989). Retrieval inhibition as an adaptive mechanism in human memory. In H.L. Roediger & F.I.M. Craik (Eds.), *Varieties of memories and consciousness: Essays in honor of Endel Tulving* (pp.283-289). Chichester, UK: Wiley.

Brainerd, C. J. & Reyna, V.F. (2004). Fuzzytrace theory and memory development. *Developmental Review*, 24, 396-439.

Bretherton, I. (1993). From dialogue to internal working models: The co-construction of self in relationships. In C.A. Nelson (Ed), *Minesota Symposia on Child Psychology*, Vol. 26. Memory and affect in development (pp237-264). Hillsdale, NJ: Erlbaum.

Bentin, S., Kutas, M., & Hillyard, S. (Feb. 1995). Semantic processing and memory for attended and unattended words in dichotic listening: Behavioral and electrophysiological evidence. *Journal of Experimental Psychology: Human Perception and Performance*, 21(1), pp. 54-67.

Bjork, J.M., Knutson, B., Fong, G.W.,Caggiano, D.M., Bennett, S.m., & Hommer, D.W. (2004). Incentive-elicited brain activity in adolescents: Similarities and differences from young adults. *The Journal of Neuroscience*, 24, 1793-1802.

Bluestein J. (2008) *The win-win classroom: A fresh and positive look at classroom management*. Thousand Oaks, CA: Corwin Press.

Cahn , B. R. & Polish, J. (2006). Meditation states and traits: EEG, ERP, and neuroimaging studies. *Psychological Bulletin*, 132(2), 180-211.

Cahill, L. (May 2005). His brain. *Scientific American*, 40-47.

Chi, M.T. (1978). Knowledge structures and memory development. In R.S. Siegler (Ed.), *Children's thinking: What develops?* Hillsdale, NJ: Erlbaum.

Cleveland E. & Reese, E. (2005). Maternal structure and autonomy support in conversations about the past: Contributions to children's autobiographical memory. *Developmental Psychology, 41*, 376-388.

Covey, S. (2004). *The seven habits of highly effective people*. New York: Free Press.

Cox, J. E. & Nelson, D. (2008). The relationship between thinking patterns and emotional skills. *Journal of Humanistic Counseling, Education, and Development*, 47 (1), pp1-9.

Damasio, A. (1994). *Descartes' error: emotion, reason, and the human brain*. New York, NY. Penguin books.

Danham, S.A., Bassett, H.H. & Wyatt, T (2007). The socialization of emotional competence. In J.E. Grusec & P.D. Hastings (Eds.), *Handbook of socialization*. New York: Guilford.

Dodge, K. (1993). Social cognitive mechanism in the development of conduct disorder and depression. *Annual Review of Psychology*, 44, 559-584.

Dweck, C. (Dec. 2007-Jan. 2008). The secret to raising smart kids. *Scientific American Mind, 43, 365-373.*

Eisenberg, N., Fabes, R.A., & Spinrad, T.L. (2006). Prosocial development. In W. Damon & R. Lerner (Eds.), *Handbook of child psychology* (6th ed.). New York: Wiley.

Eisenberg, N. & Morris, A.D. (2004). Moral cognitions and prosocial responding in adolescence. In R.M. Lerner & L. Steinberg (Eds.), *Handbook of adolescent psychology* (2nd edit), pp155-188). Hoboken, NJ: Wiley.

Ellis, D. (2007). *Becoming a master student*, 12th ed..New York: Houghton Mifflin.

Ekman, P. (2007). *Emotions revealed.* New York: Owl Books.

Ekman, P., Davidson, R., Ricard, M., Wallace, A. (2005). Buddhist and psychological perspectives on emotions and well-being. *Current Directions in Psychological Science*, 14(2), 59-63.

Ericsson, K.A., Charness, N., Feltovich, P.J., Hoffman, R.R. (EDs) (2006). *The Cambridge handbook of expertise and expert performance.* New York: Cambridge University Press.

Faber, A. & Mazlish, E. (1999). *How to talk so kids will listen and listen so kids will talk.* New York: Harper Paperbacks.

Fields, R.D. (2005). Making memories stick. *Scientific American*, 292, 75-81.

Flavell, J.H. (2004). Theory of mind development: retrospect and prospect. *Merrill-Palmer Quarterly*, 50, 274-290.

Flavell, J.H., Green, F.L., Flavell, E.R. (2000). Development of children's awareness of their own thoughts. *Journal of Cognition & Development*, 1, 97-112.

Freeman, J., Epston, D., Lobovits, D. (1997). *Playful approaches to serious problems.* New York: W.W. Norton.

Gardner, H. (1983). Frames of Mind. New York: Basic Books.

Gardner, H. (1993). Multiple intelligence. New York: Basic Books.

Goldsmith, H.H. (2002). Genetics of emotional development. In R.J. Davidson, K.R. Sherer & Goldsmith, H.H. (Eds.), *Handbook of affective science.* Oxford, UK: Oxford University Press.

Goleman, D. (1995). *Emotional intelligence.* New York: Basic Books.

Goleman, D. (2006). *Social intelligence.* New York: Basic Books.

Gottman J.M. (2008). *Research on parenting* at www.gottman.com./parenting/research.

Gurian, M. (2001). *Boys and girls learn differently.* New York: Jossey Bass/John Wiley.

Haden, C.A., Ornstein, P.A., Eckerman, C.O. & Didow, S.M. (2001). Mother-child conversational interactions as events unfold: Linkages to subsequent remembering. *Child Development*, 72(4), 1016-1031.

Hansen, R. & Mendius, R. (2009). *Buddha's brain: the practical neuroscience of happiness, love and wisdom.* Oakland, CA: New Harbinger.

Hebb, D. O. (1949). *The organization of behavior: A neuropsychological theory.* New York: Wiley.

Henderson, V.L. & Dweck, C.S. (1990). Motivation and achievement. In S.S. Feldman & G.R. Elliot (Eds.). *At the threshold: the developing adolescent.* Cambridge, MA: Harvard University Press.

Hollister Sandberg, E., Spritz, B.L. (2010). *A clinician's guide to normal cognitive development in childhood.* New York: Routledge.

Kabat-Zinn, J. (2003). *Coming to our senses*. New York: W.W. Norton.

Kabat-Zinn, J. (2005). *Full catastrophe living: Using the wisdom of your body and mind to face stress, pain, and illness, 15th ed.*. New York: Delta/Bantam Dell.

Kagan, J. (2007). What is emotion? New Haven, CT: Yale University Press.

Kohn, A. (1999). *Punished by rewards: The trouble with gold stars, incentives plans, As, praise and other bribes*. Boston: Houghton Mifflin.

Kohn, A. (2005). *Unconditional parenting*. New York: Atria Books.

Willingham, D.B. (2001). *Cognition: The thinking animal*. Upper Saddle River, NJ: Prentice Hall.

Haden, C.A. ,Ornstein,P.A., Eckerman,C.O. & Didow, S.M. (2001). Mother-child conversational interactions as events unfold: Linking to subsequent remembering. *Child development*, 72(4), 1016-1031.

Howe, M.L., & Courage, M.L. (1997). The emergence and early development of autobiographical memeory. *Psychological Review*, 104, 499-523.

Jenkins, A. (1990). *Invitations to responsibility*. Adelaid, Australia: Dulwich Centre Publications.

Joesting, L.A., Carroll, R., Faieta, D., Florence, G., Joesting, L., Martin, B., Ostach, J.,Van Hook, D., Warnemuende, M. (1995). *Communicate!* Communication Research Associates. New York: Kendall/Hunt Publishing.

LeDoux, J.E. (1996). *The emotional brain*. New York: Simon Schuster.

LeDoux, J.E. (2002). *Synaptic self: How our brains become who we are*. New York: Penguin Books.

LaMare L.J. & Rubin, K.H. (1987). Perspective taking and peer interactions: Structural and developmental analysis. *Child Development*, 58, 306-315.

Lazar, S.W., Kerr, C.E., Wasserman, R.H., Gray, J.R., Greve, D.N., Treadway, M.T. et al. (2005). Meditation experience is associated with increased cortical thickness. *Neuroreport*, 16 (17), 1893-1897.

Lewis, M.D. & Steiben, J. (2004) Emotion regulation in the brain: Conceptual issues and directions for developmental research. *Child Development*, 75, 371-376.

Malik, N.M. & Furman, W. (1993). Practitioner Review: problems in children's peer relations: What can the clinician do? *Journal of child Psychology & Psychiatry*, 34, 1303-1326.

McGaugh, J.L. (1992). Affect, neuromodulatory systems, and memory storage. In S.A. Christianson (Ed.), *Handbook of emotion and memory*. (pp245-268). Hillsdale, NJ: Erlbaum

McGuigan, F. & Salmon, K. (2004). The time to talk: The influence of the timing of adult-child talk on children's event memeory. *Child Development*, 75, 669-686.

Moore, K.D. (2005). *Effective instructional strategies: From theory to practice*. Thousand Oaks, CA: Sage Publications.

Murachver, T., Pipe, M., Gordon, R., Owen, J.L., & Fivush, R. (1996) . Do, show and tell: Children's event memories acquired through direct experience, observation, and stories. Child Development, 67, 3029-3044.

Nelson, K. (1992). Emergence of autobiographical memory at age 4. *Human Development*, 35, 172-177.

Nelson, K. (1993). The psychological and social origins of autobiographical memory. *Psychological science*, 47, 7-14.

Nelson, K. (2005). Evolution and development of human memory system. In. B.J. Ellis & D.F. Bjorklund (Eds.),

Origins of the social mind: Evolutionary psychology and child development (pp. 319-345). New York: Guilford.

Nylund, D. (2000). *Treating Huckleberry Finn*. San Francisco, CA: Jossey-Bass.

Orobio de Castro, B., Merk, W., Koops, W., Veerman, J.W. & Boscvh, J.D. (2005). Emotions in social information processing and their relations with reactive and proactive aggression in referred aggressive boys. *Journal of Clinical Child & Adolescent Psychology*, 34, 105-116.

Papalia, D., Wendkos-Olds, S., Duskin-Feldman, R. (2008). *A child's world: Infancy through adolescence*, 11th ed.. New York: McGraw Hill.

Reeder, S., Martin, T. & Turner (2010). Memory Development in childhood. In (Eds.) E. Hollister-Sandberg & B. Spritz, *A clinician's guide to normal cognitive development in childhood*. Routledge: Ney York.

Reese, E., Haden,C., Fivush, R. (1993). Mother-child conversations about the past: Relationship of time and memory over time. *Cognitive development*, 8, 403-430.

Reese, E. & Newcomb, R. (2007). Training mothers in elaborative reminiscing enhances children's autobiographical memory and narrative. *Child Development*, 78, 1153-1170.

Restak, R. (2007). *The naked brain: How the emerging neurosociety is changing how we live, work, and love*. New York: Three Rivers Press.

Reyna, V.F. & Brainerd, C.J. (1995). Fuzzytrace theory: An interim synthesis. *Learning & Individual Differences*, 7, 1-75.

Rubin, K.H., Bukowski, W., Parker, J. (2006). Peer interactions, relationships and groups. In W. Damon & R. Lerner (Eds.), *Handbook of child psychology* (6th edit). New York: Wiley.

Saarni, C., Campos, J., Camras, L.A. & Witherington, D. (2006). Emotional development. In W.D. Damon & R. Lerner (Eds). *Handbook of child psychology* (6^the edit), New York: Wiley.

Salovy, P. & Meyer, J.D. (1990). Emotional intelligence. *Imagination, Cognition, and Personality,* 9, 185-211.

Santrok, J.W. (2009). *Child development,* 12th ed.. New York: McGraw Hill

Schacter, D. (2002). *The seven sins of memory: How the mind forgets and remembers.* New York: Houghton Mifflin.

Schneider, W. (2004). Memory development in childhood. In P. Smith & C. Hans (Eds.), *Blackwell handbook of childhood cognitive development.* Malden, MA: Blackwell.

Seligman, M. E. P. (2002). *Authentic Happiness.* New York: Free Press.

Shiraev, E. & Levy, D. (2007). *Cross cultural psychology: Critical thinking and critical applications* (3rd ed.). Belmont, CA.

Siegel, D. (1999). *The developing mind.* New York: Guilford.

Siegel, D. & Hartzell (2004). Parenting from the inside out. New York: Tarcher.

Siegel, D. (2007). *The mindful brain.* New York: W.W. Norton.

Sousa, D. (2001). *How the brain learns* (2nd edit). Thousand Oaks, CA: Corwin Press.

Tannen, D. (1990). *You just don't understand.* New York: Ballantine Books.

Thompson, R.A., Meyer, S.A. & Jochem, R. (2008). Emotion regulation. In M.M. Haith & J.B. Benseon (Eds.). *Encyclopedia of infant and early childhood development.* Oxford, UK: Elsevier.

Tileston, D. W. (2004). *What every teacher should know about classroom management and discipline.* Thousand Oaks, CA; Corwin Press.

Tulving E (2002). "Episodic memory: from mind to brain". *Annual review of psychology* **53**: 1–25.

Wallace, A. (2007). *Contemplative science: Where neuroscience and buddhism converge.* New York: Columbia University Press.

White, M. (2000). *Reflections on narrative practice.* Adelaid, Australia: Dulwich Centre Publications.

White, M. (2004, October 22-23). *Mapping narrative conversations.* Presentation for Bay Area Family Therapy Training Associates, San Francisco, California.

White, M. (2007). *Narrative maps.* New York: W.W. Norton.

White, M., & Epston, D. (1990). *Narrative means to therapeutic ends.* New York: W. W. Norton.

Zimmerman, J., & Dickerson, V. (1996). If *problems talked.* New York: Guilford Press.

Acknowledgments

I am eternally grateful to all the children and adolescents who have contributed to this book by candidly sharing their stories. Their real names and identifying information have been changed to keep their identities confidential. I have thoroughly enjoyed every single one of my Skill Boosting Conversations with them and have myself learned quite a bit on how to be a kind and respectful human being.

Heartfelt acknowledgments to my editor Caroline Pincus who has provided incredible editorial support, keen advice and beyond, throughout the writing and publishing of this book. She has certainly been a most wonderful "book midwife" and has helped me navigate the tricky translation of narrative therapy jargon into more easy to read and accessible language. Many thanks also to my publisher Angela Hoy for patiently answering my thousands of questions and trying to help me with deadlines.

I feel privileged to work with Jeffrey Zimmerman, Ph.D., my BAFTTA colleague and friend, who has been so honest about loving or disliking specific sections of the draft and with whom I have enjoyed fascinating conversations on interpersonal neurobiology. I am also indebted to my narrative therapy students, pre and post-doc school counseling interns, and workshop participants around the world who have raised important questions about my work and helped me make it clearer and clearer.

This book would not have been possible without the medical support of Dr. Rick Peterson from Health Now Medical and Kathleen Kraskouskas from the Cranio-Sacral Therapy Center who helped me and my son reclaim our lives from celiac disease.

Finally, I would also like to express my gratitude to my extended family in Canada, Mireille, Marc, Frederic, Michele and Jean, who always stimulate my mind with interesting conversations. In California, I am eternally indebted to my close ones who have tolerated my regular disappearance into the office to type a few pages when the ideas bubbled in my mind. Eternal thanks to my beloved children who shared their Mommy with a computer for a year, my husband Paul who provided patient feedback and is primarily responsible for the number of stories in this book ("more stories, more stories!") and, last but not least, Francine-Esther who provided nourishments, treats, babysitting, chapter re-readings and everything an author needs to bring a project to fruition.

About the Author

Marie-Nathalie Beaudoin, Ph.D. is the training director at Bay Area Family Therapy & Training Associates (BAFTTA) in California, where she sees private clients and supervises the counseling work of doctoral and post-doctoral students in two school districts. Marie-Nathalie also teaches a number of classes such as Child Development, and Family Therapies at John F. Kennedy University in Campbell, CA. She presents internationally and has published several books, including the translated bestseller *Responding to the Culture of Bullying and Disrespect: New perspectives on collaboration, compassion and responsibility."*

In her free time, Marie-Nathalie enjoys hiking and rock-climbing with her husband Paul, and spending time with her children playing soccer, jumping on the trampoline, or creating fun art projects. You can find more information on her work at www.baftta.com. For workshops, school counseling services or consultations, you can reach her at:

Bay Area Family Therapy & Training Associates (BAFTTA)
M.N. Beaudoin, Ph.D.
21760 Stevens Creek, #102
Cupertino, 95014

beaudoin@jfku.edu

Other books by the same author:

Responding to the Culture of Bullying & Disrespect: New perspectives on Collaboration, Compassion, and Responsibility (2nd ed.)

M.N. Beaudoin & M. Taylor

Responding to the Culture of Bullying and Disrespect offers new understandings and a set of concrete conversational ideas to deal with a number of problems such as disrespect and bullying. It includes many real-life examples, stories and classroom activities. Corwin Press/Sage Publications, 2010.

Creating a Positive School Culture: How Principals and Teachers Can Solve Problems Together

M.N. Beaudoin & M. Taylor

Creating a Positive School Culture provides strategies for principals and teachers to understand, prevent and solve school climate problems. Corwin Press/Sage Publications, 2004.

Working with Groups to Enhance Relationships

M.N. Beaudoin & S. Walden

Working with Groups to Enhance Relationships offers 46 creative and fun group exercises to assist people in developing, and enriching their relationships. Whole Person Associates, 1998.

LaVergne, TN USA
18 October 2010
201324LV00003B/1/P

9 781609 104764